Jane Arnold
Herbert Puchta
Mario Rinvolucri

Imagine That!

Mental imagery in the EFL classroom

Imagine That!
by Jane Arnold, Herbert Puchta and Mario Rinvolucri

© HELBLING LANGUAGES 2007
www.helblinglanguages.com

First published 2007
ISBN 978-3-902504-84-6

The publishers would like to thank the following for their kind permission to reproduce the photographs and other copyright material:
TA FANTASTIKA BLACK LIGHT THEATRE PRAGUE - a non-verbal performance *Aspects of Alice* www.tafantastika.cz p26; **José María G. Spínola** p47, p83, p86, p103, p120, p121, p175; **Martin Cook (HumanDescent)** p65; **Herbert Puchta** p111; **Dena Arnold** p129.

Song 'Look Inside', p56, lyrics by Jane Arnold, music by David Kettlewell www.new-renaissance.net
Music for activity p118 composed by David Kettlewell
Music for activities p55, p135, p160, p173 composed by Ramón García Tamarán,
Music for activity p103 composed by Francisco Ortuño,

Edited by Caroline Petherick
Designed by Gabby Design
Cover by Capolinea
Illustrations by Barbara Bonci p33, p37, p44, p138; Alessandra Ceriani p139; Yissuko p8, p11, p14, p18, p21, p22, p57, p111.
Printed by Grafica Veneta

To the wonders of human imagination

Our thanks go to

· Caroline Petherick for editing this book with great professionalism, patience and good humour.

· Lucia Astuti and her team at Helbling Languages for their enthusiasm and support for this project.

· Michael Grinder for sharing generously during a seminar at the Hoedekenhus in Germany the outcomes of his applied research with 'at risk' students and the need to help them develop their visual thinking skills.

· Tammi Santana, Inma León and other colleagues and students for useful feedback which has helped us refine our ideas.

Contents

Contents

Introduction

I believe that much of the time and attention now given to the preparation and presentation of lessons might be more wisely and profitably expended in training the child's power of imagery and in seeing to it that he was continually forming definite, vivid, and growing images of the various subjects with which he comes in contact in his experience.

(John Dewey, *My Pedagogic Creed,* 1897)

An overview

How many windows are there in your home? If someone asked you this question, you would probably visualise your place and move mentally through each room counting the windows. Giving and receiving directions, trying to remember where we left our car keys, seeing how we want to rearrange a room without actually moving the heavy furniture – in all cases mental imagery is there to help us. In everyday life we automatically use the images in our mind in many ways as part of our natural mental processes.

Some of the greatest discoveries and contributions in the arts and sciences have been made through the use of images. Mozart visualised his compositions in his mind before writing them down on paper, and Beethoven, after losing his outer sense of hearing, created some of his finest music – which he could only have heard with the mind's ear. Kekule is said to have discovered the structure of benzene with his 'mental eye' in a daydream, and Einstein, whose basic idea for the theory of relativity came through an image of himself riding a light beam, explained that his thinking processes were not verbal but, instead, rich in images. Examples like these show that mental images are an important part of the process of creative discovery.

According to many medical researchers, we may turn to imagery to help our bodies to heal, and it is used extensively for improving performance in

almost all sports. For example, Gallwey speaks of the 'inner game of tennis':
'Take some time to imagine yourself hitting the ball with power, using the stroke which is natural to you. In your mind's eye, picture yourself serving, filling in as much visual and tactile detail as you can. Hear the sound at impact and see the ball speed toward the service court. Hold this mental image for a minute or so ...' (Gallwey, 1972: 70)

Imagery work can be used to rehearse and improve many skills, and it is involved in many fields such as science education, computer graphics, and bio-medicine. Mental images are inseparable from information processing and information storage, the bases of learning; their importance for education is undeniable. According to Alesandrini (1985:207), 'the question is no longer whether or not mental imagery facilitates learning but rather how it can best be used to produce the optimum facilitation'. In the ELT classroom it can help us to teach better and our learners to learn more effectively. Earl Stevick stresses that language and mental images are intimately tied up with one another. He points out the importance of images for verbal communication: 'an exchange of words is communicative only when it causes some modification of the images in the hearer's mind' (Stevick 1986:16).

To talk about mental images the term *visualisation* is often used. Here we shall be considering it as the process of forming and using mental images for some purpose, of creating what has been referred to as 'movies-in-the-mind'. Often connected to our emotions, it refers to perception coming not from outside stimuli but from inside our mind. Our mental images are in no way limited only to the visual, but also include the auditory, tactile, kinaesthetic, olfactory, and gustatory. Try for a moment to hear the Happy Birthday song with your mind's ear or touch velvet with your mind's fingers... or smell freshly baked bread or taste a lemon.

Words are, in a very real sense, glued to images. If someone tells us not to think of elephants, as we hear these words, the opposite inevitably happens; we get a mental picture of an elephant.

This connection is bidirectional. Words can stimulate images in our minds, and when we have a mental image, we can label or describe it verbally.

There are very solid reasons for dealing with imagery in language teaching. Imagery work can contribute significantly to our students' language learning in direct or indirect ways. It can, among other things:

· increase learners' cognitive skills and their creativity
· improve their reading and listening comprehension
· provide things they want to say when they speak or write
· enable them to remember better what they have learnt
· enhance their motivation
· strengthen their self-concept, and
· help to focus their attention.

Charles and Jill Hadfield (1998:11) point out how imagery work could even be used to enrich learning contexts with few material resources: 'Use the limitless resource of students' imagination ... simply get the students to close their eyes and imagine their own pictures which become the stimulus for speaking or writing activities'.

In this book we will be exploring how the ELT classroom can be enriched by the incorporation of activities using mental imagery, the inner resource that Majoy (1993:64) sees as being 'one of the most powerful, effective and necessary tools for teachers'. In the introduction, after looking at some of the relevant background information about mental imagery, we offer some practical suggestions about beginning to use imagery activities in your classroom. The main part of the book consists of five sections:

Section 1, **Visualisation Training**, will give you suggestions for beginning to work with imagery and for helping learners who have difficulty visualising to do so better.

Section 2, **Language in Mind**, focuses on specific aspects of language or the learning process.

In Section 3, **Stories Stories Tell**, we'll explore ways images and stories can be used in the classroom.

The activities of Section 4, **Images of Time and Space**, revolve around these two concepts, and

Section 5, **Spinning Inward**, has an emphasis on the learners themselves.

The CD-ROM and the Helbling website provide, between them, a wide variety of material for use with the activities, including original music, art, photos, worksheets, and taped guided-imagery scripts. See inside back cover for information about using the CD-ROM and the website.

Mental images and cognition

The neurologist Antonio Damasio explains that images are what 'mind' is actually made of. He says that as complex organisms, human beings 'generate internal responses, some of which constitute images (visual, auditory, somatosensory, and so on), which I postulate as the basis for mind'. He goes on to state that an essential condition for mind is 'the ability to display images internally and to order those images in a process called thought' (Damasio 1994:89-90) Mental imagery, then, is an important part of who we are and how we use our brain effectively. Not surprisingly, it is also an important area in neuroscientific research.

The connection between cognition and mental imagery is not a recent discovery. Philosophers from Plato through William James and down to the present have stressed the importance of imagery for our thinking processes. Kosslyn, director of the image laboratory at Harvard University, states that 'a thorough review of the history of imagery would in fact be a history of most of psychology' (Kosslyn 1980:438). Scientific interest has been heightened through work in neuroscience, where imagery is 'one of the first cognitive domains to be firmly rooted in the brain' (Kosslyn et al 1995:1336).

Aristotle affirmed that it is impossible to think without a mental picture, and we know today that learner cognition will indeed be supported if the use of mental imagery is promoted in the classroom. As research indicates, our ability to create meaning from oral or written language is greatly dependent on the images formed. Language comprehension, then, will not only depend on learners' good decoding or vocabulary skills but also in part on their ability to create and use mental images which will enable them first to understand texts in the foreign language better and later to recall more information from these texts. Individuals, however, differ in their ability to form mental images, so we can contribute to successful language learning if we help students to use more effectively their imaginal resources. It has been shown that students who are able to generate a lot of images perform better on memory tasks. What is particularly interesting for us as teachers is that students who generate only few images can be taught to develop their imagery faculties, and when they do so their scores on these tasks improve. In fact they can achieve results similar to those of students who are high image generators.

One factor that drastically undermines cognitive efficiency is lack of attention. Many of our students today are brought up on a steady – and unhealthy – diet of extreme visual input, generated externally through video games, computers, and hours and hours of television. This may include an increasing amount of multitasking where they may be involved with several types of media at the same time. Research has shown that this can lead to serious problems with attention, which in many cases are being dealt with basically by drugging attention-deficit students. Though the habits developed by dealing with this bombardment of stimuli may prepare young people for similar-type activity later in the workplace, Wallis (2006) points out that cognitive scientists are alarmed by current trends, and that we know from research how 'one's output and depth of thought deteriorate as one attends to ever more tasks'. It is often the case that students even become uncomfortable if there are pauses in this constant stimulation. The brain, however, needs time for consolidation of information coming in through the senses. Imagery work in the classroom can be used first as a way to connect with students who have become accustomed to this high external visual exposure and then to give them a chance to go inside, to extend their attention span and to become more centred and clear-thinking.

Mental-imagery work can facilitate memory for language learning and use
Damasio (2000:107) points out that language 'is a translation of something else, a conversion from non-linguistic images which stand for entities, events, relationships and inferences'. Given that language learning and use is one of our most significant mental processes, it is not surprising that imagery should be involved in diverse ways. One key aspect is memory, and imagery can help us to reconstruct in the present what we experienced and learned in the past. From classical times, the mnemonic function of imagery has been recognized and used extensively. More recently, in the latter part of the 20th century, numerous experiments have proven that subjects learn and remember material that is concrete (imagery-related) better than that which is abstract.

Work in cognitive psychology provides strong evidence of the importance of imagery in language processing. Paivio's Dual Coding Theory posits that we have two processing systems, verbal for language items and non-verbal for images. As Sadoski and Paivio (2000) have pointed out, these two processing systems organically influence one another both in language reception and in recovering it for production. As we process information coming in from our senses and convert this sensory information to language, we rely greatly on our imagery system. The connection of words with experience and with emotional responses to experience gives words their meaning. In our classrooms, language learners will first understand and then remember better if they make more connections among all the elements involved: experience-emotions-images-language.

The process of learning a foreign language becomes more efficient if students create as many direct associations between the target language and their knowledge of the world as possible. As with the process they went through when learning their mother tongue, Italian students of English, for example, who manage to associate *tree* with the image of a tree rather than with the Italian word *albero* will be able to apply what they have learnt faster and more efficiently, since they do not have to go through a process of translating the word from mother tongue when they are in a situation where they need it.

In his discussion of the relationship between the dual coding theory and second-language learning, Paivio (1986:352-3) summarizes:

'A major implication is that it is especially important to learn the second language (L2) in direct association with appropriate nonverbal referents because such referents (objects, events, behaviors, emotions), cognitively represented, constitute the knowledge of the world that L2 must tap if it is to be used meaningfully. The richer and more direct the referential connections, the more efficient L2 use will be.'

Mental-imagery work can facilitate reading and listening comprehension
The importance of reading and listening comprehension for language learning is certainly a given today. Through exposure to the language in the form of comprehensible input, learners are able to internalise language elements and, in time and to different degrees, acquire the language. This is the process which permits human beings to acquire

their first language, and it is of great significance for us in language teaching. Speaking of first-language learning, Zimmerman and Keene (1997) explain how proficient readers naturally create mental images out of their previous knowledge – from all five senses and also from their emotions – while they read and after reading. In learning a second language, visualisation is also a strategy used by good readers.

Studies in neuroscience have clear implications for the EFL classroom, as they indicate that imagery plays a vital role in the comprehension of language. Kosslyn et al (1995:1340) stress that our faculties for imagery and words 'work together in many ways ... imagery can help one to learn new information, including verbal information. In addition, imagery can help one to comprehend verbal descriptions'. Extensive research has been carried out on how mental imagery can improve comprehension and recall, both in L1 and L2. This influence can be explained in large part because language material is processed more deeply through the use of imagery and is stored in a more permanent manner. In fact, we could say that images are essential for us to get meaning out of language. Images help us to construct meaning from texts and it has even been said that 'those who cannot imagine cannot read' (Eisner 1992:125).

Reader–response theories reaffirm what many teachers observe: reading is an experience which readers create. If learners are passive agents, they are not really reading. Their active participation can be encouraged with the use of mental images. Stimulation of imagery already in their mind before reading can help learners increase both enjoyment and comprehension of new texts, especially with narrative texts. In other words, when our students read or listen to a story in English, they will be able to comprehend the gist of the story better if during the reading or listening process they are able to build a full representation of the story in their mind. This process works best when it includes the creation of a 'story space' (where the story is set), with visual images of the people and object in the story, with auditory representations of people's voices, environmental sounds and so forth. Often, the reader will also 'move around' in that space, feel imagined body sensations (e.g. when the text is about someone running in the rain), or even imagine the smell or taste of things suggested by the mental representations.

Mental-imagery work can provide rich stimuli for speaking and writing
A common complaint of students regarding using the target language either for speaking or writing is that they don't have anything to say. One of the most important points about imagery work in the ELT classroom is that it leads naturally to text production. With learners of all ages it can encourage more fluent speaking with learners focussing on meaning (see Activities 15 and 73). When teaching writing, if we tell students just to write a story or a description of something, writer's block may take over and little will get produced. However, if we stimulate diverse sensory images in their minds before they need to begin writing, the results are inevitably richer (see Activities 45 and 66). Imagery work can lead to greater fluency in both speaking and writing, because if students have something in mind they want to say, they are freed from the need to find

a message to deliver, and can proceed to trying to find ways to express it. Mental-imagery activities provide students with a greater feeling of being in control, because what they are going to produce in the target language is stimulated not only by an external verbal source, which they may not comprehend fully, but also by their inner images of diverse sensory types.

In a discussion of her work as a writing teacher, Susan McLeod mentions the importance of visualisation, which seems to be a part of intuition, one of the sources of creativity. She notes that after using a guided visualisation with one class for their final assignment, 'Rod', not a natural writer, wrote with great intensity; his paper was the best he had done that year and, unlike previous ones, needed very little revision. After writing, he commented that 'he "knew" how this paper should go right from the start – it just "flowed"' (McLeod 1997:88). Good writing depends to a large extent on having something to write about, and imagery work provides learners with rich, meaningful content.

Mental-imagery work can enhance students' motivation and strengthen self-concept

The effectiveness of instruction in any academic context depends to a great extent on learners' motivation, and it is indeed essential for language learning. Work with images in the ELT classroom can increase students' interest and bring them into a more active and participatory relationship with the material at hand (Tomlinson and Avila 2007a and b). For example, much of the enjoyment that narrative texts bring the reader is through the mental imagery which naturally develops in our mind as we read, creating a greater sensory and emotional reality. Learners can be encouraged to try to see images as they read texts in the target language similar to the way the read in their first language. Also, when working with texts, we can give preference to questions of an open-ended nature where learners' mental images can be a springboard for greater engagement.

An important component of motivation is personal meaning. Dörnyei (2001:63) points out that 'one of the most demotivating factors for learners is when they have to learn something that they cannot see the point of because it has no seeming relevance to their lives'. Images, however, are always related to personal meaning, as they come from within us as we read or listen. Often when we read a novel and then see a film based on it, the film is disappointing, in part because when we read we create our own images, and these are deeper and richer for us. In the classroom, imagery work makes our learners protagonists of their learning process. For example, to bring classroom texts closer to students, Dörnyei (2001:64) suggests having them 'imagine how a particular theme from the coursebook could be transferred to locations and situations associated with their own life experiences' [our emphasis].

In their study of aspects of psychology that affect language learning, Williams and Burden (1997:206) stress the importance of self-concept: 'An individual's self-concept will have considerable influence on the way in which he or she learns'. Learners with a low self-concept regarding the L2, who think 'I can't learn English', need help in breaking this negative idea, which is limiting their real ability. If we as teachers just tell them 'You can learn English', this will probably go in one ear and out the other. However, if we really want to help them to strengthen their self-concept, it is likely to be more effective to have them experience success in inner images with a visualisation activity where they can 'see' and 'feel' themselves solving learning problems and speaking English well, especially if activities of this nature are repeated. Brown (1991:86) suggests students try what he calls the visualisation game: 'Visualise yourself speaking the language fluently and interacting with people. Then when you are actually in such a situation, you will, in a sense, have "been there" before.'

 In a similar way, Dörnyei (2005) in his discussion of motivation and self-motivation presents the concept of the ideal language self. He explains that if in your ideal vision of yourself there is a facet associated with knowing the L2, this can act as a strong motivational force. Using this concept and writing about Willingness to Communicate (WTC) in a foreign language, Yashima, Zenuk-Nishide and Shimizu (2004:143) ask an interesting rhetorical question: 'Is it possible to hypothesize that learners who clearly visualise 'possible' or 'ideal' English-using selves are likely to make an effort to become more proficient and develop WTC and engage in interaction with others using English?' So in our classes we can try to ensure that knowing English seems both attractive and possible for our students, thus helping them to access a future image of themselves as successful speakers (see Activity 67).

Related to self-concept is the process of goal-setting. If students are encouraged to set language-learning goals which are within their reach, to design plans for reaching these goals and then to create a mental image of themselves achieving the goals, this can provide a powerful source of energy for learning. In a sense, our images can take us where we want to go.

Notes from the authors

Jane Arnold

As an educator influenced by humanistic teaching orientations, I feel a responsibility to try to contribute to the development of learners' full potential, and I originally became interested in imagery as a way to do this. At the University of Seville in Spain, I have been involved in research projects dealing with mental imagery as a useful tool for the language-learning process. In one study (Arnold 2000), we wanted to explore the use of relaxation/visualisation techniques to deal with anxiety in listening comprehension exams, since students constantly complained that their results were worse than they should have been because the exam situation made them nervous. The study was done with two groups of students who had expressed anxiety and who volunteered to try to work with the problem. Both groups were given a pre-test, six practice exams, and a post-test over a period of two months. However, for the experimental group before each practice exam there was a pre-listening activity consisting of two parts, an initial relaxation exercise and then, in this state of relaxation, a second part designed to bring about attitudinal changes through visualisations. Different types of visualisations were used to help the students learn to access guidance from within themselves or to gain confidence by acquiring a more positive attitude towards themselves and their abilities to understand spoken English.

In the study, the experimental group showed greater improvement in the practice exams than did the control group. Comments from students in the experimental group on a final questionnaire showed that they experienced much lower levels of anxiety: '*I have learned to understand the whole text. I can only do this if I am relaxed. Now I have time to think*'...'*I think being calm is very important because the texts are accessible in terms of vocabulary and the rest; we only have to recognize what we already know*' ... '*I try doing these exercises at home. They are useful in any situation*'... '*Do I understand the texts now better than before? Of course!*'

One student commented in an interview after the experiment:

Instead of hearing words in English and trying to translate into Spanish and memorize as before, I started seeing the text in images, as if I was watching a film or as when you are a child and you listen to a story. At the time I didn't know why, but the images gave me confidence in my ability to listen better. (Nuria)

In a different exam situation, I remember the case of 'José' who could not pass the oral exam which was a requirement for the second-year language course at the University. He had tried three times already with the same result: a fail. Finally, the exam topic he drew was one he was passionate about and one for which he had a rich bank of images in his mind. His exam this time was much better than the level needed to pass because, though his language skills hadn't changed significantly, he was now able to use them efficiently.

In other aspects of the learning context, I have continually been surprised by the increase in creativity and productivity when activities with imagery have been used.

Herbert Puchta

I first came across the idea of using visualisation by chance in the middle of a lesson teaching English to 11-year-olds in their first year of learning. I was working with a textbook that had my learners practise dialogues based on a weather chart giving the weather conditions in various towns for the previous ten years or so. The students were supposed to work in pairs and ask each other questions like *What was the weather like in Moscow on the 16th July 1987?* with each partner answering based on what they could find in the weather chart.

The activity went all right, but I felt that the students weren't really interested in what was going on and neither was I. Watching them, I noticed that they were mechanically doing what I had told them, but nevertheless seemed to be far away. *Where are they? DAYDREAMING! Why not try to exploit what is going on in their minds anyway?* What I did was to have them leave the textbook exercise that was not related in any way to their reality and to go deeper into their daydreaming.

I asked my students to put their heads down onto their desks, resting on their arms, and to close their eyes if they wanted. They looked at me in surprise. *Really? Yes. Just relax. Let's have a nice break.* I waited a bit and then I started, in a very soft voice:

While you're resting on your desk with your eyes closed ... just listen to whatever you can hear ... the noise of the cars passing by ... the singing of the birds from the tree outside the window ... and whatever you can hear from within the classroom ... just relax and feel fine ... maybe you can also hear your own breath ... as you breathe in now ... and as you breathe out ... and maybe you want to come with me ... on a holiday ... it is your own holiday ... so I don't know where you're going ... while you're listening to my voice ... go on a holiday ... wherever you want ... I have no idea where you are ... maybe you are in a very warm country at the seashore ... or in the middle of the high mountains ... and I have no idea where you are in your holiday at the moment ... maybe in your room at the hotel ... or in a tent ... or maybe somewhere out in the open ... and I have no idea what the weather is like ... as you are now looking up towards the sky ... maybe you can feel the temperature on your skin ... I don't know if there is any wind ... and I'll give you a little time to enjoy your holiday fully ... now ... (silence of about half a minute) ... and now I'd like you to come back to this classroom again ... very slowly ... and open your eyes again.

One after the other the students opened their eyes again. Their faces told me that they had obviously enjoyed the little daydream. It was now up to me to turn the nice 'change', as the students would call the fantasy later when we talked about it, into an efficient language activity suitable for the level of my learners. I wrote down the following prompts on the board:
In my fantasy I was in / at / on ...
With me there was / were ...
The weather was ...
The temperature was ...
I really liked ...

Five minutes later, after I had explained the language on the blackboard to my learners and shown them how they could use the prompts in order to report about their fantasy experiences, they were fully involved in telling me and the other students in class about their 'holidays':

S1:   I was in Africa.
HP: In Africa – tell me about it.
S1:   The weather was fantastic. It was very hot. The temperature was more than 50 degrees centigrade. And I go swimming every day.
HP: Were you alone?
S1:   No, my parents and my friend was with me. He and I had a surfboard and we ... erm ...
HP: You rode it?
S1   Yes, we rode it every day ...

Mario Rinvolucri

Back in the 1970s, I was lent a book by Gertrude Moskowitz: *Caring and Sharing in the Foreign Language Classroom*. Moskowitz advocated using relaxation techniques and then leading students on dreamy walks through forests, up mountains and down to the coast. I was amazed; the coursebooks I was using in those days offered my students nothing more than 'useful', 'realistic' listening conversations in restaurants, station announcements and the like. With hindsight it meant that my students had to listen to voices they had no rapport with, and often to poorly written dialogues and gobbets of prose.

But Moskowitz was suggesting that students create their own mental scenes from just a few well-chosen words spoken by their teacher, with whom they had a real relationship.

I tried out some of the guided visualisations she proposed and was amazed to hear just how powerfully and individually the students reacted to my words. I was delighted, but in the late 70s I was not yet ready to accept that fully unleashing language students' creativity was one of the fastest, most efficient and most pleasurable way of having them absorb and use new language.

Over the last 25 years I have benefited from the influence of two master teachers, John Morgan, who wrote *Once upon a Time* with me, and Bernard Dufeu, author of *Teaching Myself*. John's way of telling stories had the entrancing quality of good guided-imagery work: he used few, but well-chosen, words, he used silences masterfully, and his voice seemed to be within you without your knowing how it had got there. Bernard's teaching method, *Psychodramaturgie Linguistique*, is based on relaxation, the teacher-student relationship, mutual trust and the awakening of students' imagination. So I have gradually come to realize more fully the power and usefulness of working with guided imagery, as illustrated within the pages of this book; I hope that you and your students will derive not only significant learning but also great enjoyment from it.

Getting the most out of imagery in ELT

The image is the great instrument of instruction: what a child gets out of any subject presented to [them] is simply the images which [they themselves] form in regard to it.

John Dewey, *My Pedagogic Creed*, 1897

There are some preliminary issues that it may be helpful for you to consider before beginning to work with imagery in your classroom.

First of all, creating a relaxed state in which students are centred can bring many benefits to the classroom. (To give students the possibility of enjoying a moment of quiet transition as class begins, see below: **Helping students to 'arrive' in the 'here and now' of the language class**).

Then there is the question of eyes open or closed. Though when working with imagery it is generally most effective to close your eyes, as students are often not used to doing this in class it is best not to insist on it at the beginning. We can at least ask them look down so they can concentrate better, and later suggest they try closing their eyes to see their inner images better.

Finally, visualisation activities are best introduced gradually with teenagers and adults. Young children have a rich IMAGE-ination, but unfortunately schools tend to push out images to make way for words and numbers, as students are pressured to do well in exams which measure verbal and mathematical intelligence. Yet, as Howard Gardner (1993) has shown, success in life depends on many different intelligences, all of which can provide support for learning a second language (see Puchta and Rinvolucri 2005 for ways to use the Multiple Intelligence framework in ELT). One of the different intelligences Gardner discusses is the spatial intelligence, or the visual/spatial as it is sometimes called. It involves 'the capacities to perceive the visual world accurately, to perform transformations and modifications upon one's initial perceptions, and to be able to re-create one's visual experience, even in the absence of relevant physical stimuli' (Gardner 1993: 173), in other words, to visualise. To the detriment of the imagination and creativity, this ability, so useful for many reasons, is not stimulated in the classroom, and so learners become unaccustomed to working with their imaginal faculties. However, we can try to bring images back into the picture in ways that are easily accepted. (See the suggestions below and Section 1 for activities to develop the students' ability to visualise better.)

Imagery in Language Learning – Multiple Uses

Imagery work is relevant for all areas of language learning. There will be good listening practice when you lead guided visualisation exercises, and many of the activities suggested here integrate the different skills. For vocabulary learning, we can teach learners what research has proven to be one of the most effective strategies: associating words with images. Many studies have shown that concrete words are nearly always easier to learn because they can be associated with an image. In this vein, Stevick (1996: 122–3) speaks of the use of the keyword or 'key image' technique. He cites the case of English speakers trying to learn the German word for egg, *Ei*. As the pronunciation is similar to the English word *eye*, they could associate an image of a fried egg as an eye with eyelashes as a memory help.

English spelling is a difficult area for many learners. For working with words that are often written incorrectly, Revell and Norman (1997:41) suggest the following: write a word high up on the board or on a card held high enough that the students must look up to see it, tell them to blink their eyes as if taking a *mental* photograph, then with eyes closed, see the 'photograph' of the word in their mind and finally write the word from memory. To test if they really know it, they can bring it up in their minds and try to spell it backwards.

Grinder (1991:118) offers a somewhat similar technique for learning spelling. Write a word on the board and underline each letter:

t h r o u g h

Then the students look at the word, memorising each letter and its place in relation to the other letters. You erase just the letters, leaving the dashes (_ _ _ _ _ _) and then point to each dash in order, having students call out the appropriate letter. When they seem to have it learned, the same can be done, but mixing the order in which the dashes are pointed to.

With grammar, images can help us 'get a feel' for verb tenses. Take a basic sentence and get students to imagine it: *I'm eating a chocolate chip cookie (ice cream, sweets, an apple ...).* Then modify the verb tenses and get the students to continue seeing the action in their minds. *I've eaten ..., I've just eaten ..., I eat ..., I don't eat ..., I'm going to eat ..., I wish I hadn't eaten so many ...* and so forth. This gives grammar a reality not possible in many typical textbook exercises.

For work with pronunciation, Adrian Underhill (1994) suggests *internal imaging.* Say the word or phrase to be practised once, and then ask learners to hear it internally in your voice ... then in theirs ... then whisper it ... and finally say it aloud. This gives them the opportunity to work with the language with their mental ear, to make a useful auditory image of it before having to produce it orally.

Brian Tomlinson (1994) uses what he terms *Total Mental Response*, a type of activity that often involves movement and gives learners time to process language internally in images before speaking. To do this, read aloud a text with a lot of actions and have the whole class act it out. For example, the whole class stands up in one part of the room and you say the following, getting them to act out what you say: *Everyone was at the beach ... some people were swimming ... near the water, some children were playing ball ... some were eating and drinking. One young woman* (here you describe one of your students who will do the action) *picked up a seashell she found and ...* etc. When the text is finished, students are asked to play it back in their minds, and then you give the beginnings of sentences or phrases – *Everyone was ... Some people were ... some children were ...* – and encourage the students to shout out the completions. An example of this type of exercise can be found in Activity 40.

One listening and speaking activity that never fails to involve students is the following. As if telling a story, say something like this:

Claudia was looking out the window at the street below. The only sound was the rain on the window. A tear fell from her eye; she looked at her watch and went to sit down on the sofa. She sighed, and another tear fell. Finally, she heard steps approaching. The door opened and Jeremy entered ...

Wait a moment and then begin to ask questions like: *How old was Claudia? What was she wearing? What colour was her hair? Was it long or short? What was in the room? How tall was Jeremy? What happened when Jeremy entered?* The first question may confuse students who are used to parroting back words they hear – and in this case you are asking for information that's not in the spoken text. But when they discover that the answers come from the story that they have been creating in their mind's eye, they begin to participate very actively. There can also be a writing follow-up where students continue the story they began in their minds. In a similar way, whole classes together can construct elaborate stories from their mental images. One of the advantages of speaking activities of this nature is that students needn't fear giving a wrong answer. They are speaking about their mental picture, and they know what they want to say.

More and more teachers are concerned with value-based foreign language teaching. If we, for example, aim at developing our students' empathy, their ability to put themselves in other people's shoes, we can ask students to try to imagine what it is like to be another person, e.g. the protagonist of a reading or listening text: *What do you do when you get up in the morning? Where do you go? What happens during your day? How do you feel about your life?* If disadvantaged individuals or groups are the focus of the text, this can also help to raise students' social consciousness.

Guided-imagery exercises which take students to different places and situations are useful for many purposes in the language classroom, and are also very enjoyable. On these mental journeys, learners may travel anywhere, from a simple visit to the room they had as a child to more complex journeys such as meeting with a wise person (see Activity 70). The level of the students permitting, these should be done in the target language. However, for less proficient learners the exercises can also be done in the L1, to lead afterwards into L2 activities with the imagery that has been produced. Tomlinson and Ávila (2007a) point out that learners generally lack a rich, multidimensional representation of the world in their L2, and so they feel that some use of the L1 can be permitted in order to generate interesting ideas to talk or write about in the target language.

Helping students to 'arrive' in the 'here and now' of the language class
We are not always aware of all the extra baggage our students bring into the classroom – problems at home, worries about their future, insecurity caused by low self-esteem and a long etcetera. We may have an excellent lesson planned and great teaching skills, but if a student has just had an argument with a friend, he or she is not going to be in an adequate state to learn. This situation can be changed noticeably if we use a combination of relaxation and imagery activities to help them 'get fully into class' before we begin teaching what we plan to teach. Also, after a very active

phase of our class, we may want to change the atmosphere. By helping students to relax and slowly shift their attention from the outer world to their inner perceptions, we make it possible for them to calm down, to become grounded. After tiring activities or those that don't engage students, imagery work can also help them to regain lost energy and attention. Although imagery exercises have an inner focus, many of them lead to very interactive work and have a positive effect on the group dynamics (see Activities 50 and 75).

The following are a selection of short activities to be done one at a time to accustom students to get into a more receptive state of mind for learning and to see some simple pictures in their minds. Ask students to sit comfortably. They can close their eyes if they want to. Then suggest they do one of the following brief activities. If learners are at a low level, you can use their L1. In a quiet voice, give them one of the following instructions:

· *Think of a place you know that is quiet and pleasant. Remember in detail what it looks like ... what sounds you might you hear there ... See yourself there ... What are you doing? ... Is anyone with you?... How do you feel? ...*
· *Think of a word you really like in English ... Play with the word in your mind ... Hear the sound of it ... See it written on the board, in your notebook, or elsewhere ... Imagine it written in gold letters, make it bigger, make it smaller ... See pictures of it or related to it ...*

· *Remember a day when you felt really happy. You have one minute to relive it in as much detail as possible.*
· (Play some quiet, relaxing music; take your pick from the CD.) *Listen to the music, let images come freely into your mind as you hear it.*
· *You are going to think in English for one minute. Try to think only in English. Think of words, phrases. You don't need to think in complete sentences. Maybe words for things you see in this room. Maybe words you have learned recently. Maybe different categories of words, like animals, colours or clothes. You can repeat some words if you want. Just try to stay with English for one minute.*
· *I am going to tell you when a minute starts and ends and I'd like you to count how many breaths you take in the minute.* (One minute.) *Now I will do the same, but try to breathe a little slower and to take at least one less breath this time.*
· *Sit with your hands in your lap. I am going to say 'Start' and you are*

going to try to guess when a minute has passed. No watches allowed. When you think the minute ends, put your hand on your desk. Start. (Watch them, and after about 70 seconds tell the class who was able to guess the minute exactly. If they want to try again, repeat the exercise.)
· *Imagine a bird. What colour is it? Where is it? Put the bird on a rock ... behind a rock ... in a tree ... See it flying in the sky. Where does it fly now?*
· *See a scene from a favourite film, one that you remember well ... Who are the characters? ... What happened before this scene? ... Watch it for a few moments ...*

As a follow-up, you can, if you wish, have a class discussion of the activity the students have done, or in twos or threes they can briefly tell each other what they imagined or experienced. If you often use exercises like this to begin class, students can keep a special page in their notebooks to write down a short comment about each one as soon as they finish. This centring diary can be written in their L1 and can best be done not as part of work required for a grade. The total of three or four minutes spent in all can change a chaotic atmosphere into a space for productive work.

Getting into visualisation

Classroom experience and research show that students who are able to think visually are often the ones who achieve better academically. The main reason for that is that in test situations, visual students tend to remember information more precisely and are able to recall data stored in their brains faster than the more kinaesthetic or auditory types. Therefore, without being any more intelligent than more auditory or kinaesthetic students, visually strong learners usually achieve far better results. Michael Grinder (personal communication) uses the following metaphor to explain why this is the case.

The very visual student

The very auditory student

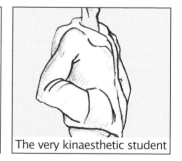
The very kinaesthetic student

According to Grinder's metaphor, very visual students have 'a camera instead of a head', which means they are good at 'taking pictures of what they see' and storing information in their 'mind's eye'. These students will be able to recall information very precisely, and quickly, when needed.

Very auditory students, however, tend to remember what they 'have recorded' (i.e. what they have stored on their inner cassette player through rote learning). When it comes to remembering, their brain often works in a way similar to the way we go backwards and forwards in order to find a particular piece in a tape on a cassette player without a counter: they find it difficult to quickly find a piece of specific information. An example would be a very auditory student giving a presentation (after they have practised it well by saying it aloud to themselves several times).

When interrupted midstream (e.g. when someone asks a question), they often seem to be lost when, after answering, they want to carry on with their presentation. They need to go back to the beginning and – if they can – 'fast forward', in order to be able to carry on with their talk.

As for very kinaesthetic students, they 'have no head at all', which does not mean that they are less intelligent, but that their main input channel is their bodily, kinaesthetic, one. They need to have 'hands on' learning experiences, and will remember best what they have learnt through movement, touch, interaction, group work and role play, whereas they find it very difficult to store and precisely recall information that is presented to them mainly or exclusively in visual or auditory ways.

Research shows that very kinaesthetic students, although often extremely creative and intelligent, are frequently found among those students who are generally described as being 'at risk'. So teachers who are aware of this often try to teach in multi-sensory ways, thus appealing to all three sensory types. This is especially important since we, as teachers, tend – often subconsciously – to prefer presentation techniques that are in line with our own learning-style preferences. In other words, teachers who are rather visual will tend to use lots of visuals in their own teaching; their board work will look very neat, and they will use colour underlining, colour coding, drawings, graphs etc. All this is excellent for the visual students in class – but it might not be so helpful to those students who find it difficult to remember information visually.

Apart from developing foreign-language skills, and helping develop the students' visual memory, the activities in Section 1 can also have a very facilitating effect on the students' ability to focus their attention. These activities are built on two key principles:

a) the principle of synaesthesia
In order to help highly kinaesthetic students develop their ability to store visual information in their memory, we are well advised not to start in the visual-sensory domain – which is their weakest – but to start from their kinaesthetic strength, and gradually lead into the visual area. The principle of synaesthesia is easy to apply. For example, if it is difficult for a student to look at an object and remember later what it looks like, the student could first be asked to touch the object, and feel its texture (a kinaesthetic approach) and while they are doing this, they could be asked to gradually become aware of the object's colour, shape etc. Later, when the student is to recall the colour or shape of the object, they can first of all be asked to remember the feeling of holding the object in their hands and remember feeling its texture, and while they are doing this to gradually *get a sense* of the colour and shape.

We should like to point out here that asking non-visual students to remember what things *looked* like often gets reactions like 'I can't remember', whereas they are much more at ease when the teacher uses kinaesthetic or sensory-neutral language, as in the example above where the students are asked to *get a sense* of the colour of the object rather than *to see it* in their minds' eye.

b) the 'easy-on-content' principle

Michael Grinder warns of teaching a new process (such as learning to visualise) alongside teaching new content. He stresses the need to use content that is already familiar when we guide very kinaesthetic students towards learning to visualise. Hence with activities such as those in Section I, beginning to use visualisation exercises, it is important for the teacher to make sure that if the students are not already familiar with the language – both vocabulary and constructions – they carefully pre-teach it. So these activities are ideal for use in language revision.

Likewise, kinaesthetic students won't learn to develop their visual thinking skills through a one-off activity. Teachers who work regularly on the development of students' visualisation skills in their classes report that students' memory skills tend to improve significantly with time, and that the activities also have a very positive effect on the students' ability to focus their attention and concentrate on their work.

Learning to visualise: helping students who think they can't

There are usually a few – and not only very kinaesthetic – students in a class who claim that 'they can't see anything' when the teachers ask them to close their eyes and see pictures. This is an interesting phenomenon, since when you ask the same student to close their eyes and imagine that they are opening the door to their house with their key, and then ask them to imagine the colour of the door, they will probably be able to tell you the colour of the door later, but at the same time might claim that they didn't see it in their mind's eye, or only got a sense of the colour.

As one reader of the manuscript of this book commented, it seems that the problem of 'not seeing' is rather compounded. In the words of this colleague:

'For me perhaps the problem is even generated by the use of the word 'see'. I am mainly verbal/auditory, and so I take 'see' literally, and try and use my eyes. But of course this doesn't work, however hard I try! I have often talked about my difficulty in visualising, and when I've brought this point up, the reaction has fairly frequently been:

"But of course. That's why you can't. You're trying too hard!" '

People who try to force themselves to SEE mentally often believe that the picture has to be almost like a projection on the inner part of their eye lid, and they try very, very hard to see it, but that does not get them the desired results. In order to see pictures, they need to be relaxed and wait for the pictures to come, rather than try to produce them.

Michael Grinder's explanation is that those people's brains work so fast that they see pictures only for a very short period of time, and hence 'have an intuition' of an image rather than seeing the image. In his words, it is the teacher's task to help those students 'stabilise their intuition'. Other experts, like the authors of *The Mind Gym: Wake your Mind Up* (2005, p. 232), claim that 'some people think they can't visualise. This is, of course, nonsense. It's just that they suppose that visualisation is more complicated than it actually is. At its simplest, visualisation is simply imagining something that isn't there in front of you. It does require some effort, more than say, watching a film, which is an almost entirely passive experience, but it is not difficult'.

The same authors also give a number of 'rules' that should be applied (*The Mind Gym*, 2005, pp. 232-233):

1. No distraction – getting your students to be calm and focussed and to close their eyes helps them to visualise better.
2. Use better breathing – better breathing helps students to relax, and the more relaxed they are, the easier it is for them to visualise.
3. Involve all senses – although the technique is called visualisation, it is really also about sound, touch, taste and smell. The more senses are involved, the easier it is for students to imagine things.
4. Include emotions – especially positive ones.
5. Practise – as with most things, our ability to visualise will get better with time and effort.
6. Be patient – in many ways, we can't force visualisation to happen; it takes time and at first may feel a little awkward and clumsy. Tell your students to be patient – and to persevere.

To get started you might want to try some simple exercises like the following:
· *Open your book to page 54* (or any page not yet studied, preferably one with several pictures). Give them only one or two seconds to look at it then say: *Close your book. What was on the page? Try to see it in your mind. Compare what you remember with your neighbour.*

· Get the students to read a short text, either from a chapter in their coursebook not studied yet or a photocopy. Ask them to close the book or turn over the photocopy. Ask questions like the following, appropriate for the specific text: *See the text in your mind. Where was the name of the character first mentioned – at the beginning, middle, or end of the text? What was the first word of the text? How many paragraphs were there? Did the last sentence end with a question mark, an exclamation mark or a full stop? Was the illustration on the right or the left side of the page?* If you wish, repeat with a similar text to see if they get a clearer picture of it this time.

· Explain to your students that you are going to give them a sentence and ask them to add words to it according to what they see in their minds. Say, or write on the board, a sentence like the following: *A girl is walking down the street.* Then say: *See or get a sense of the girl. What is the girl like? Add one or two words to describe her. How is she walking? What is the street like? Where is she going? Why is she going there?*

· Working in pairs, students make a simple drawing of a place they know well (e.g. their street, a part of the city, a room in their house, a holiday spot) or a place they invent. Student A shows their drawing for about 15 seconds to Student B, who makes a mental photograph of the drawing; without looking again at the drawing Student B then tries to recall it and describes it back to Student A. Reverse roles. Explain to students the benefits of developing the ability to see pictures in their minds and tell them they can practise doing this by taking mental photographs at any time; all they have to do is look at something, close their eyes a moment and try to get an image of it in their mind and then open their eyes to check how well they could see. The more they try it, the easier they will find it.

· Say to your students in a quiet voice: *See a black curtain in a theatre … Against the black curtain see a bright butterfly flying around … Now see a little girl in a blue and yellow dress … She is jumping and skipping … She has a butterfly net in her hand. She runs after the butterfly and tries to catch it … Does she capture it in her net? … Continue to see the black curtain, and now a circus clown appears in a red and green suit … What is his hair like? … His nose? … Are his shoes big or little? … A little boy in a blue and white striped shirt appears. He shakes hands with the clown … The clown jumps up and down because the boy has a buzzer in his hand which gives the clown a shock.* (You have just treated your students to an inner performance of the Black Light Theatre of Prague. You can easily invent other imaginative scenes for your students with, for example, people flying or riding bicycles in the sky. Anything is possible.)

You may wish to use these simply as brief listening activities to help students develop or strengthen their ability to engage with their mental images. However, many can be followed with an interactive activity in which they tell a classmate what they saw, or one where they write about it.

See Section 1 for more ways to help those students who think they can't visualise to learn to do so.

A summary of general guidelines for work with mental imagery in the EFL classroom

Introduce imagery activities very gradually, trying first some of the short options above. Explain to your learners why you are using a different type of activity from what they normally do in their coursebooks; tell them that these activities will help them to learn better, and let them have fun at the same time.

Encourage them to close their eyes if they want to. At first this may produce some resistance so you could start with a very quick activity: If you have a lesson on means of transportation, for example, say: *You have only three seconds. Close your eyes and see a car and afterwards tell me what colour it is. Ready, get set, go.* (3 seconds). *Open your eyes.* You can adapt this process to many different situations.

When you ask for feedback or discuss one of the activities with the class, it may be a good idea to call first on stronger students who are well liked and who you observe enjoying the activity. Tim Murphey (1998b) has developed the concept of near-peer role modelling – we often model our behaviour and beliefs on those of others who we see as similar to us, and so if certain students express positive attitudes towards something related to the class, other students may follow their lead.

Practise the instructions you will be giving during visualisations. What you say should not sound hesitant and uncertain. However, be sure to include the intentional pauses at the appropriate places, to give learners time to activate their images and develop them. Prepare a script of what you will say and when you will pause, if you feel this will help. We have generally given suggestions with the activities both as to the language and the pauses (...). How long you pause will depend on your class and what seems right for them; generally two or three seconds is enough, but if the exercise is more complex, longer pauses may be appropriate. You need to be sure to give your students time to form the images. At the beginning you may want to use the recordings of the scripts on the CD directly in the classroom or as a guide for your own preparation before class. When using the CD, where *Pause* is indicated in the script, stop the CD player for a moment.

Consider your learners' level of comprehension when you prepare scripts, and, though the guided visualisations can be excellent listening practice, tell your students that they needn't try to understand everything, just follow the general idea.

Practise reading your scripts aloud before using them in class; and consider practising with a colleague. Whenever you say a script to students, use a quiet voice, speaking fairly slowly and without too much inflection. Stand up straight and don't move around a lot, or gesture, while you speak.

To help students get clearer pictures, give them clues. If you ask them to visualise a tree, ask: *What kind of tree is it? Is it big or little? Does it have leaves or not?* Bring in all the senses – not just sight, but hearing, touch, smell and taste – when you can, since multi-sensory imaging will lead to richer activities.

When the exercise is coming to an end, bring students back to their normal awareness gently. If they are very involved, you might say *When I count from one to five, return to this room, feeling relaxed and alert. One ... two ... three ... four ... five.* Or simply say in a quiet voice, *When you are ready, open your eyes,* or *Very good.* Find what feels best for you.

Be ready to adapt any of the activities you use so they will have the best possible results with your particular groups.

Whether you are doing an imagery exercise related to something in your coursebook or as a free-standing activity, there should be a clear purpose and some follow-up; this can be either simply talking about what they experienced or setting a continuation writing or speaking assignment. At all stages of a task, imagery can be useful: before the task to activate previous knowledge or create new combinations of images and ideas to use, during the task to connect more deeply and directly, and afterwards as a memory prompt or as a stimulus for further work. It is also useful to remind students often to use their mental images, to open their mind's eye, whenever they read or listen to texts, because benefits are cumulative.

Last but not least: two ways teachers may use imagery.

Scott Thornbury (1999) speaks of an image-based approach to class planning. If we develop mental scripts of a lesson's overall shape, we can plan lessons more coherently. We 'see' the lesson before we begin; in images – seeing, hearing, sensing kinaesthetically – we experience its parts, and can generate more ideas, pace it better, anticipate and solve possible problems that might come up.

One of the factors that determines the effectiveness of our teaching has to do with the images that we have of ourselves. Our self-concept, the way we 'see' ourselves as teachers, is a good starting point for reflection. Perhaps you might want to try the following:

When you are alone and in a quiet place, relax your body and your mind and visualise a scene; it is a typical class, a few good things, some less good. Problems come up; there are no very effective solutions ... Everyone is anxious for the class to be over and to go home. When the bell rings, there is a rush for the door... Now, change the scene. You are teaching the best class ever. Everyone is enjoying themselves. The students are learning a lot, both about the language, which they are using enthusiastically, and about themselves and each other. There are many positive feelings toward the experience, and when the class is over you and the students take a pleasant sensation out of the classroom. (Arnold 1999:276)

Two situations, two images. If it's the second one that you choose to keep in mind, you are one step closer to being there.

SECTION 1
VISUALISATION TRAINING

1 Point to Where the Window Is

Language focus: Lexical set of words relating to the home

Level: Elementary and lower intermediate

Time: 5–15 minutes

Preparation: None.

in class

1. Pre-teach words for objects in a room (*table, chair, door, window, carpet, curtains, lamp, walls, window sill, cooker, fridge, sink, cupboard, wardrobe, chest of drawers, bed, bedside table, sofa, armchair, bath, mirror, shower, toilet* etc.)

2. Ask your students to take a book – the thicker, the better – and hold it on their lap. Ask them to touch all four sides of it. As they are doing this, ask them to pretend that the four sides are the walls of their room:
   As you are touching the four sides of the book, I'd like you to pretend that this is not a book, but your bedroom. And I'd like you to pretend that the four sides are not the sides of your book, but the walls in your bedroom.

3. After a few seconds …
   Now touch where the door to your room would be. Touch that spot. Now use your fingers to walk from the door to the bed. Touch where the bed is.

4. After a few seconds …
   Now touch where the window is … and if there are more windows, touch where the other windows are … Now walk with your fingers from one of the windows to the light switch … touch the light switch … imagine that you are turning on the light … imagine you can hear the sound of the switch being turned on … Now walk to all the other objects in your room that you haven't touched yet … maybe there is a chair … and a desk … a carpet … curtains … Take your time … touch all the objects in your room.

5. Later, students can be asked to write a short text describing their room. It might be necessary to pre-teach prepositions and language of description.

Variation
1. If the activity is done several times with the same group of students, vary the content by asking them to imagine other rooms (their living room, their kitchen, the classroom, the school hall, a shop etc.).

2. Teach a different lexical set, e.g. for rooms in a house, get students to imagine their house or flat, and touch different rooms, but also include instructions like 'Walk downstairs', 'Walk upstairs', if there is a staircase in their house/flat, 'Walk out the door,' etc.

3. The activity can also be done in pairs with students taking turns telling each other which objects in their room to touch.

4. When you have done the activity several times, extend it by asking your students to close their eyes after some time, and imagine that they are touching the different objects in the room they have chosen and, as they are touching the different objects, to get a sense of their colour(s).

5. Tell students to imagine their home. Ask them to see it in their minds and mentally walk through all the rooms. Have them draw a floor plan of their home, adding a sketch or words for the important pieces of furniture in each room. Then they mentally hide a small object somewhere in the home, writing the place down on a piece of paper which they fold so the hiding place can't be seen. In pairs, As tell Bs what object they have hidden and Bs try to find out where it is: *Is it under the bed? ... Is it behind the sofa? ...* When they guess, the Bs 'hide' their object for As to find.

Note
The main purpose of this activity is to help very kinaesthetic students who find it hard to visualise to develop their visual memory in a process of synaesthesia (by starting in their strong kinaesthetic domain and gradually leading over to their visual domain). For best results, variations of the activity can be done repeatedly.

Acknowledgement
We learned Variation 5 from Javier Ávila.

2 The Kitten on your Lap

Language focus: Basic animal vocabulary, language of imperatives

Level: Elementary to advanced

Time: 5–10 minutes

Preparation: None.

in class

1. Pre-teach any of the following words that your students may not be familiar with: *cat, kitten, fur, paws, purr, tail, head, lap* (your own, for a kitten to sit on), *stroke, touch, turn around.*

2. Sketch a cat on the board and revise the words listed above. Ask students in turn to come to the board and mime the verbs. Then get the whole class to mime or act out the verbs *stroke, touch* and *purr.*

3. Ask your students to sit with their eyes open or closed. If they want to leave their eyes open, they should 'stay with themselves' for some time and not look at what other students are doing during the activity, or talk to them. Tell them that you will ask them to imagine there is a little kitten on their lap, and you will ask them to imagine they are stroking it, and they should actually do what you ask them to do.

Now, with your eyes open or closed, feel the warmth of the kitten on your lap. Imagine you are gently touching the kitten's head now. Start exploring the kitten's head. Touch its little ears gently ... now start stroking its fur ... very gently ... stroke the kitten's fur ... and as you are doing this, imagine that the cat starts purring ... it likes your strokes ... the cat starts purring ... feel the vibration of the cat's purring ... and as you can feel it, imagine that you can also hear it ... take your time ... enjoy stroking the cat's fur ... and keep listening to its relaxed purr ...

Now you notice that the kitten is standing up on your lap ... carefully move your hands back ... and watch the kitten as it turns around ... and then sits down again on your lap ... now the kitten's head is on the other side ... gently touch the kitten's head again, and start stroking it ... feel the warmth of her fur ... and notice the purring ...

Variations

1. The activity can be used with other types of pets – depending on the kind of the pet, ask your students to imagine that they are standing next to it (though they should stay seated).

2. Some of your students might prefer an activity where you ask them to imagine having their bike standing next to them. Get them to touch the handlebar, the saddle, and any other parts your students can understand. Finally, say something like:

   Okay, if the bike has a saddle, wheels and handlebars, it must have a colour too. When you open your eyes, turn to your neighbour and tell them what colour the bike is. Then describe as many other details as possible.

Note

It is interesting to watch the students' reaction during the activity when you tell them that the cat on their lap turns around and sits down again with its head facing the other way. If students then change the direction of their strokes too, it is a fair indication that they really are visualising the cat on their lap.

3 Questions about a Picture

Language focus: Present progressive, action verbs

Level: Elementary to advanced

Time: 15 minutes in each of two lessons a week apart, plus homework between the two

Preparation: Prepare a picture and a set of questions, or photocopy the worksheet (p. 37).

in class

Lesson 1

1. Give each student a photocopy of the worksheet on p. 37 for this activity. Ask them to fold it along the dotted line and look at just the picture part. Draw the grid below on the board, and ask the students to call out words from the pictures. Write their words in the grid, and elicit any other words from the pictures that the students have not mentioned.

Animals	People	Actions

2. Ask the students to look at the pictures for a minute and remember as many details as possible. Then tell them to turn the picture part of the worksheet face down, and look at the questions. Ask them, working in pairs, to read the questions and find out which of them they can answer without difficulty – and without turning the worksheet over!

3. Check with the students which of the questions they have found the most difficult to answer. Elicit the answers to those, and get students to check them against their pictures.

4. Tell them that their homework is to study the picture at home for at least 3 minutes every day during the following week. Demonstrate the following to your students: read Question 1 aloud, check the picture for the answer, close your eyes, and tell your students that you are imagining seeing that part of the picture with your eyes closed. Tell them to do the same with the remaining questions.

5. To attract their interest, tell them that in a week's time you are going to give a fun quiz in the class that will prove to them that they can't answer even half your questions about details in the

picture. Announce that your questions could be about all kinds of details, not just about the questions on the worksheet; give one or two examples from the list in Lesson 2.

Lesson 2

1. Give students a minute to look at the picture again. Then ask them to put the picture out of sight, and get them to brainstorm words from it.

2. Ask the first question from the bottom half of the worksheet. When a student has given you the correct answer, ask for a show of hands and write the number of correct answers on the board next to the number of the question. Continue like this with the other questions.

3. Then proceed with further questions about details in the pictures. For example:

What's the dog sitting on the clown's bike holding?
Is the dog on the clown's bike looking in the same direction as the clown, or in the opposite direction?
What's on Claire's T-shirt?
What's on Sandra's T-shirt?
What colour is the dog that's chasing Mr Farrows?
What's the dog holding in its mouth?
Ms Woods has got a plaster cast. Is it on the left or the right foot?
What's she wearing on her head?
What has her headgear got on it?
Next to Ms Woods there is an animal. What kind of animal is it?
What's the animal next to Ms Woods doing?
What's Mr Brown wearing on his head?
Who's wearing shorts – James or Amy?
There's an animal sitting on top of Mr Brown's car. What kind of animal is it?
What's the animal sitting on top of the car saying?

Note

This activity is very motivating, since students normally get far more correct answers than what the teacher had predicted in order to challenge them. At the same time it offers good memory training.

3 Questions about a Picture

Worksheet

Clair

Sandra

Mr. Farrows

Ms. Woods

Joe's home made ice-cream
Simply the Best!

This is fun!

Mr. Brown

James Brown

Amy Brown

Questions:

1. What animal is there on the luggage rack of the clown's bike?
2. What are the names of the girls playing football?
3. What's the goalkeeper's name?
4. What's Mr Farrows doing?
5. What animal is running after Mr Farrows?
6. What's the name of the woman wearing big sunglasses?
7. What's she doing?
8. What's Joe doing?
9. What does the slogan on Joe's ice cream stall say?
10. Who's pushing Mr Brown's car?

4 Come to your Senses

Language focus: Lexical area of the senses, speaking

Level: Elementary to advanced

Time: 20 minutes

Preparation: None.

1. Write the names of the verbs of the senses on the board like this:

see	hear	touch	taste	smell

2. Ask students to brainstorm things they like in each category and write these down under the appropriate verb. (Lower-level students can suggest words in their L1, to be written up in English.) Add a few items of your own, perhaps of a more complex nature (*bread that is baking in the oven ..., raindrops falling on the roof ...*). When you have a good list, erase it all.

3. Pair students randomly. Have them sit or stand together and tell them they are going to give each other gifts for each of the five senses. Tell them they can use some of the things suggested earlier, but they should try to think of some new ones to give, as well. They begin with *see*, and each gives an image to the other, using their name each time. Let them know that they can take their time to think of images to give, and to enjoy the images they are given. You may want to demonstrate first with a volunteer:
A: '*B, I want you to see a garden of flowers. It is a nice sunny day.*'
B: '*A, I want you to see a mountain with snow.*'
A: '*B, I want you to hear a piano.*'
B: '*A, I want you to hear children playing in a park and laughing ...*'

4. When everyone has given and received all five senses, have them discuss the following with their partner:

Which image could you visualise most easily? Tell me some details about it. What feelings did you have about it? Were there any images that you couldn't visualise?

5. This activity can be repeated, changing pairs, or done again another day.

4 Come to your Senses

Note
With any learning, information comes to us through our senses. Meaning comes to us through our experience of the sensory world, yet schooling tends to emphasise words and concepts, and sweep the sensory experience under the carpet. Bringing it back into the classroom can enrich and strengthen learning.

Acknowledgement
Similar work on developing an awareness of our senses through visualisation can be found in Houston (1982), Murdock (1987) and Whitmore (1986).

From Touch to Inner Picture

Language focus: Nouns

Level: Elementary to advanced

Time: 3–5 minutes

Preparation: None.

1. Ask your students to work in pairs. In turn, they will put their right hand on the desk, palm down. Tell them to imagine that the back of their partner's right hand is a notepad. Then tell them that they're going to make imaginary drawings on their partner's hand.

2. Student A thinks of a noun that can be expressed by a picture, then 'draws' the noun on Student B's hand, using their index finger. Student B, eyes closed, is to guess what the word is, but should not say the word aloud.

3. When Student B believes they have recognised the word, they write it in capital letters on the back of Student A's hand. Tell them that they should write the word in letters each one of which is big enough to cover the back of the hand, and on top of the last letter. If Student A 'reads' the word correctly, they swap roles, but if not, they start again.

Variations
1. Student A 'writes' the infinitive of an irregular verb (in capital letters) on B's hand; B writes the past form of the same verb on A's.

2. Students 'draw' or 'write' on each others' backs.

Note
This activity is in many ways prototypical of the process that helps strongly kinaesthetic students best in learning to visualise. When Student B feels an imaginary item being drawn on their hand or their back, they focus on their strong (kinaesthetic) sensory channel. In order to be able to recognise the image or word, they then have to translate the kinaesthetic sensation into a picture. Maria Montessori used this principle in a perfect way when teaching spelling to children, by getting them to write difficult words in sand, and remembering the letters while they were feeling the sand with their fingers.

6 From Movement to Inner Picture

Language focus: Using movement to help memorise language

Level: Elementary to advanced

Time: 5–10 minutes

Preparation: Select a poem that can easily be mimed, or use the poem here.

Lesson outline

1. Pre-teach any necessary language so your students can easily understand this poem:

   A box full of chocolates!
   Hip, hip, hooray!
   A box full of chocolates
   is my prize today!
   Triangles and circles, rectangles and squares –
   from the box into my tummy!
   Chocolates!
   Yummy!

2. Ask your students to stand up, and listen to you and copy your movements. Then recite the poem, accompanying each line with the following movements:

A box full of chocolates!	Use your hands to 'draw' the outlines of a box in the air, and make a movement with one hand to suggest that the box is very full.
Hip, hip, hooray	Raise both hands in a gesture of triumph.
A box full of chocolates	Repeat first-line mime.
is my prize today	'Draw' a circle on your chest as if indicating a medal there.
Triangles and circles, rectangles and squares –	'Draw' a triangle, a circle, a rectangle and a square.
from the box into my tummy!	Point at an imaginary box in front of yourself, then towards your stomach.

| *Chocolates!* | Point at the imaginary box of chocolates and blow a kiss in its direction, to indicate that you love chocolate. |
| *Yummy!* | Rub your tummy to indicate that you have eaten the chocolates and are very happy now. |

3. Ask them to repeat the movements, together with you, silently; this time, you too mime the movements, without speaking!
4. Ask them to listen to the poem one more time, this time with their eyes closed, and to do the movements as they are listening. Recite the poem.
5. Finally, ask them to do the movements together with you one more time, and this time to repeat the rhyme aloud while they are doing this. But this time you speak only if the students get stuck; in most classes, it will be possible at this stage to elicit the whole text through movement without you speaking at all.

7 Internalising a Poem in Three Ways

Language focus: Internalising the language of a poem

Level: Elementary to advanced

Time: 30–40 minutes

Preparation: Prepare a poem or use the one presented here; you will need to make 2 sets of photocopies of part 2 of the poem growing line by line as described in 5 below.

in class

1. Use drawings and mime to teach any words or phrases from the poem you have selected. If you are using the poem below, these might be, for example:

   caterpillar, crawl, top of the tree, leaf, take a nap, cocoon, cosy, sleepyhead.

2. Say the words, and get your students to point to the drawings and/or mime the words. Then ask them to close their eyes and listen to you saying the words while they imagine the respective picture for each word, and remember or do the mime.

3. Present the first half of the poem in the way described in Activity 6, From Movement to Inner Picture. Mime the lines of the poem in the following way as you say them, and ask your students to listen and at the same time do the mime with you.

A little caterpillar crawls to the top of the tree.	Hold up one arm, make a crawling movement with fingers of other hand as if a caterpillar was crawling up your arm.
'I think I'll take a nap,' says he.	Make a gesture indicating that you have a great idea, and then put your hands together and, closing your eyes, briefly rest the side of your head on the back of one of them.
So – under a leaf he begins to creep	Hold out palm of one hand horizontally (the 'leaf'), and make crawling movements with fingers of other hand towards the underside of the 'leaf'.

| to spin a cocoon. | Make spinning movement with finger   underneath the 'leaf'. |
| Then he falls asleep. | Put your hands together and repeat the 'nap' mime, but hold it for a little longer. |

4. Read out the whole poem to the students:

The Caterpillar
A little caterpillar crawls to the top of the tree.
'I think I'll take a nap,' says he.
So – under a leaf he begins to creep
to spin a cocoon.
Then he falls asleep.
All winter he sleeps in his cosy bed
till spring comes along one day and says,
'Wake up, wake up, little sleepyhead.
Wake up, it's time to get out of bed.'
So he opens his eyes that sunshiny day.
Oh! He's a butterfly
and he flies away.

5. Fix 7 pre-prepared slips of paper, evenly spaced apart, onto the two side walls of the classroom. The first slip contains the first line of part 2 of the poem:
All winter he sleeps in his cosy bed

The second slip contains the first and the second lines:
All winter he sleeps in his cosy bed
till spring comes along one day and says,

The third slip contains the first three lines, and so on until the seventh slip contains the whole of part 2 of the poem:
All winter he sleeps in his cosy bed
till spring comes along one day and says,
'Wake up, wake up, little sleepyhead.
Wake up, it's time to get out of bed.'
So he opens his eyes that sunshiny day.
Oh! He's a butterfly
and he flies away.

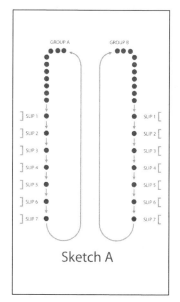

Sketch A

6. Divide your class into two groups. Group A queues up in front of the first slip of paper on one wall, group B at the other wall (see Sketch A).

Ask the first student in each queue to go to the first slip, and study the line on it carefully. Model how she should say it to herself sub-vocally several times, and then repeat it with her eyes closed.

When the student can remember the line well, she moves on to the next slip of paper, and studies the two lines on that paper in the same way, before going on to the next paper slip. In the meantime, the second student in each queue moves forward and he starts studying the first slip.

Explain to the students that when they have finished with all the paper slips they should test themselves and decide whether they want to start queuing again, or (if they feel they've remembered all the lines well) to sit down.

7. When all your students are back in their seats, ask them to dictate the poem back to you, line by line. As they dictate it, write a skeleton version of the whole poem (containing only the first letter of each word, except 'th' for 'the') on the board:

A   I   c   c   t   th   t   o   th   t
I   th etc.

8. Ask your students to work in pairs and 'read out' the poem to each other, using the skeleton text on the board.

9. Challenge your students by deleting one letter from each line, and asking them to 'read' the poem again; then delete another letter etc. until finally the students 'read out' the whole poem with all the letters removed from the board.

Notes
You should find that your students will be able to 'read out' the poem flawlessly, with many of them showing eye movements as if reading it from somewhere 'up in the air'. This is a clear sign that they have internalised the poem visually.

This activity is very well suited for working with children.

Acknowledgement
The caterpillar poem is from *Hand Rhymes*, p. 28, collected by Marc Brown, Scotprint Ltd, Musselburgh, First published 1985 by William Collins, Sons & Co Ltd.
The skeleton technique was first used by Morgan and Rinvolucri in *Once Upon A Time*, Cambridge University Press, 1983.

8

Seeing Colours and Numbers

Language focus: Colours, numbers, parts of the body

Level: Elementary to advanced

Time: 5–10 minutes

Preparation: None.

1. Ask your students to take a deep breath and then exhale very slowly. Ask them to repeat this several times, and notice how they start becoming more and more relaxed.

2. In a calm and quiet voice, say:
   Close your eyes. Imagine you can see the colour red, and the number 7. If it is difficult for you to really see the colour red and the number 7, let go and relax; just pretend that you can see them. Feel how your head and your face relax.
   Now imagine the number 6 and the colour orange. Feel how your shoulders and your chest relax.
   Imagine the number 5 and the colour yellow. Feel how your tummy and your thighs relax.
   Imagine the number 4 and the colour green. Feel how your feet relax.
   Imagine the number 3 and the colour blue. Feel how your whole body is relaxed.
   Imagine the number 2 and the colour pink. Feel how your mind is relaxed. You are completely calm now.
   Imagine the number 1 and the colour purple. You are now completely relaxed. Mind and body. Completely relaxed. Completely … relaxed.

3. Give your students time to open their eyes at their own pace.

Note
The activity draws on visual elements that students are very familiar with – colours and numbers. It is well suited to get those students who claim they cannot see pictures in their mind's eye to get into a relaxed state about not seeing pictures, and acting 'as if' they could see them.

SECTION 1: VISUALISATION TRAINING

Getting a Picture in Mind

Language focus:	Writing descriptive statements and questions
Level:	Elementary to advanced
Time:	20–30 minutes
Preparation:	Computer projection of two paintings, or a collection of cards with paintings, one for each student.

in class

1. Have students get into pairs and decide who will be A and who will be B. Project the slide of Painting 1 and have the A students study it very carefully for 3 or 4 minutes, trying to remember all the details. Meanwhile, the Bs are also looking at it, to write three true/false statements and two open-ended (*What ...? Who ...?* etc) questions about the painting.
2. Then take the painting off the screen and the Bs ask their questions. The As try to remember the image of the painting to answer the questions. When they have finished answering, let them see the picture of their painting again.
3. Repeat the process with Painting 2, the Bs studying the painting and the As writing the questions.

Variation
This can be done handing out a card with a painting to each student. After the specified time As turn their card over and Bs ask the questions they have written. Then they both work with the other card.

Painting 1

Painting 2

10

Your Own Name

Language focus: Relaxed listening, language of comparison

Level: Elementary to advanced

Time: 15–20 minutes

Preparation: Optional: bring in a CD player.

in class

1. Ask your students to sit in a relaxed way, and either play CD track no. 1 or, in a quiet voice, say:

I'd like you to focus on any sounds you can hear in this room at the moment ... the sound of (fill in with any sounds you and your students can actually hear, e.g. footsteps from people walking down the corridor ... the cars passing by in front of the windows ... the birds singing from the trees opposite the school ... etc).

For a moment, focus on your breathing ... as it comes and goes ... just observe your own breathing ... do not make it faster or slow it down ... just notice your breathing, and notice how you may already be a bit more relaxed now ...
Imagine that on the floor in front of you there is your bag ... What colours can you see? Is there a handle on it? If so, what does it look like? Is there a lock on the bag? If there is one, what colour is it?

Imagine that you open your bag now. What does it feel like to open your bag? Take out your favourite pen now. Imagine you are holding it in your hand. What temperature is it against your skin? How heavy is it? What does it feel like?

Now take your pen and write your name on a piece of paper. What does doing this feel like? How does the pen move over the paper? Is it a smooth glide, or do you feel any friction?

What do you hear as you are writing? What colour are you writing in? And what does your name look like? Are you writing in capital letters, or in joined-up script? Are the letters big or small? Do you like what your name looks like, on the whole? What parts do you like about it?

Now imagine that you put the pen into your other hand. How does it feel to hold the pen in that hand? How is it different from the previous experience? Now write your name again. What does it feel like? How does the pen move over the paper now? Is it a smooth glide, or do you feel any friction? How is the movement different from when you used your other hand?

Your Own Name

What do you hear as you are writing? What colour are you writing in? And what does your name look like? Are you writing in capital letters, or in joined-up script? Are the letters big or small? How does your name look different from the name you wrote with your other hand?

Take your time to slowly open your eyes again and come back fully to the classroom. You can do this by slowly counting with me down from ten to zero. When I have arrived at zero, please open your eyes again, and stretch and take a deep breath and look around yourself. Ten ... nine ... eight (count down to zero).

2. Ask your students what they noticed. Ask them for any visual images they saw, and whether these were clear and colourful, or black and white, or very blurred, or whether they could only sense the colour of their pen and the look of their handwriting.

Variation
Suggest to your students that they are standing in front of the door of their home. Ask them to touch the door, then the door handle, ask them for the temperature of that and then suggest that they should imagine taking the key in their hand. Tell them they should put the key in the lock, and turn it. As they are turning the key, ask them what they hear. Ask them to push the door open, and enter. Ask them what the room is like that they have just entered, what temperature they can feel in that room etc.

Note
This activity offers a good example of synaesthesia, starting with kinaesthetic experience and moving towards visualisation. Depending on the level of your students you might need to adapt the actual wording of the activity to your students' needs. One way of doing this would be to skip the more difficult passages in the activity, e.g. *How does the pen move over the paper now? Is it a smooth glide, or do you feel any friction?*

Acknowledgement
The idea for the variation comes from *The Mind Gym: Wake Your Mind Up*, p. 232, Time Warner Books, 2005.

11 Washing your Hands

Language focus: Relaxed listening, language of narration

Level: Upper intermediate and advanced

Time: 20–30 minutes

Preparation: Optional: bring in a CD player.

in class

1. Pre-teach any words that your students might not be familiar with. Tell them to sit in a relaxed way, and either play CD track no. 2 or say, in a quiet, calm voice:

Close your eyes or look into the distance. Imagine that you are in your bathroom. You are standing in front of the wash basin.

Imagine the tap, or taps, and a bar of soap. Look at the shape of the basin. Touch it with your hands. Notice what its surface feels like. Notice its temperature. Notice its colour.

Now look at the soap. What colour is it? What shape has it got?

Now put the plug into the plughole. Turn the taps on. Listen to the sound the water makes as it runs into the basin. The water is slowly getting higher. How does the sound change? Look at the place where the water flowing from the tap meets the water in the basin. What does it look like?

Before the basin gets full, turn the water off.

Now put a hand into the basin. Is the temperature okay for you? If it's too hot or cold, turn a tap on again until the temperature is right. Put both hands in the water. How does the water feel against your skin?

Now pick up the soap. How does it feel? Bring it up to your nose and smell it – what's the smell like?

Now start washing your hands. Notice the foam the soap makes, notice the sounds you're making. Carry on washing your hands. Then put the soap back on the edge of the basin, and put your hands into the water. Notice how the colour of the water changes. Are there any bubbles on the water?

Pull out the plug. What does it sound like? What does it look like when the water runs out of the wash basin? Now take a towel and dry your hands. What does that feel like? Bring your hands close to your face and smell them.

Slowly open your eyes and come back to the classroom.

Variations

1. You can extend the activity into a narrative chain, e.g. *the soap slips out of your hand and falls onto the floor. You try to pick it up, but the soap shoots out of your hand again and lands in your living room ...* Then ask the students to continue the story in their own imagination.

2. Put a short list on the board of simple activities your students might be accustomed to doing (get up and get dressed in the morning; write and post a letter; go to buy fruit ...). Have them write a short text along the lines of the one above for one of the activities (*Imagine you are buying some fruit in a shop ... Look at the different colours. Ask for what you want. As you take each piece of fruit, notice how it feels ...*); help with any language needed. In pairs, students read their text to their partner, who tries to imagine it as vividly as possible.

Note

This activity is an ideal follow-up to Activity 10, Your Own Name. Again, it's about a routine that the students are familiar with, but is richer in its sensory activation.

Acknowledgement

The idea for this activity comes from *The Mind Gym: Wake Your Mind Up*, p. 234, Time Warner Books, 2005.

12 Your Very Own Inner Film Centre

Language focus: Language of narration

Level: Intermediate to advanced

Time: 30–40 minutes

Preparation: None.

in class 1. Tell your students that they are going to do an activity that will help them to relax deeply. Ask them to find a comfortable sitting position. Then say, in a quiet, calm voice:

Take a slow, deep breath. Pause for a moment. Breathe out slowly, and notice how your chest and tummy relax. Keep breathing in this way ... until you feel quite calm and relaxed. As you are beginning to become more relaxed, notice how your breathing has become calmer and more regular.

Feel your feet firmly on the ground. Say quietly to yourself: 'My feet are relaxed. They are more and more relaxed. My feet are deeply relaxed.'

In the same way, go through the whole of your body. Say the following sentences to yourself after me, and feel how they help you to feel even more relaxed:

My arms, hands, wrists and fingers are relaxed. They are more and more relaxed ...

My shoulders, my neck, my head, my forehead are relaxed. They are more and more relaxed ...

My nose, my ears, my lips and my mouth are relaxed. They are more and more relaxed ...

My tongue, my eyes and my cheeks are relaxed. They are more and more relaxed ...

I am enjoying being more and more relaxed. I am more and more relaxed ...

I'm relaxed.

Pause for a minute or two. Then continue:

12 Your Very Own Inner Film Centre

Imagine yourself in a lift now. The lift is going to take you down ten floors. As you go down each floor you will feel even more relaxed. Imagine that you can see a number 10 in front of you. You are on floor number ten.

Now the lift starts going down.

You see number 9 on the screen. You are on floor nine ...

You see number 8 on the screen. You are on floor eight ...

You see number 7 on the screen. You are on floor seven ...

6, you are calm and relaxed

5 ... 4 ... 3 ... 2 ... 1...

You are now very calm and very relaxed.

Imagine that the door of the elevator opens. You are in a room now. It's dark and comfortable. On the wall in front of you, you can see a large screen.

There is a comfortable chair in front of the screen. Sit down in it.

Say to yourself: 'I am deeply relaxed. My mind is open and curious. I can look at the screen and see images on it. I can watch the images come and go, as I wish, or I can hold them. I can take my time now to watch the images.'

2. Give your students some time. Then carry on with your prompts: *It is now time to stand up from your chair and go back to the lift again. Watch it as it goes up from floor to floor:*

   1 ... 2 ... 3 ... 4 ... 5 ... 6 ... 7 ... 8 ... 9 ... 10 ... Take your time to open your eyes. Now stretch and yawn, and enjoy the fact that you are feeling energised, healthy and strong.

3. Ask students to work in pairs, and talk about how they experienced this activity.

Acknowledgement

This is an adaptation of an activity in Mike Samuels and Nancy Samuels, *Seeing With the Mind's Eye: the History, Techniques and Uses of Visualization*. Random House: The Bookworms, 1975, p. 152.

13 The Dreamer within Me

Language focus:	Language of sensory perception
Level:	Intermediate to advanced
Time:	20 minutes
Preparation:	Bring in a CD player.

in class

1. Write the word *daydream* on the board. Ask your students to give you words that come to their mind when they think of daydreaming, and note all these words down on the board, too. You are likely to get words like: *holiday, beach, sea, girlfriend, boyfriend, happy, island* …

2. Then lead a whole-class discussion on the topic. Use questions such as:
   Do you all daydream? Who thinks you don't daydream at all?

   When do you usually have your daydreams?

   Is there any place that you feel is especially good for daydreaming? What's this place like?

   Do you have daydreams at school? In which lessons? Do you sometimes have daydreams in the English lesson? What do you dream of then?

   When you daydream, do you see in colour, or in black and white?

   Do you hear anything during your daydreams? If yes, what can you hear? Voices? Music? Natural sounds? What else?

   Can you taste or smell anything in your daydreams?

3. Tell your students that you are going to ask them a series of questions. In a quiet voice ask these questions, and give the students about half a minute's silent time after each question.

   Can you imagine holding a red apple in your right hand?

   Can you see it now?

   Close your eyes for a minute.

   Can you see it better when you close your eyes?

   Can you feel it too? What does it feel like if you touch it?

Can you imagine taking a big bite from it?

Can you hear a sound while doing so?

Are you aware of the taste?

4. Have a discussion of your students' experiences. Usually students respond very positively to this activity because it involves several main sensory areas (seeing + feeling + hearing + tasting).

5. Then explain to your class that you want to do a daydream–like activity with them. Inform them that they don't need to try hard to see things in their mind's eye. Tell them that they should become aware also of any smells, tastes, sounds and feelings in their daydreams.

6. Play some music, and give your students time to relax and dream. Later, ask them to sit in groups and discuss what was easy or difficult for them about the activity, and why they enjoyed or didn't enjoy it.

Note
This activity is aimed at making students aware of their abilities to get different types of sensory image. It directly addresses and activates the part of our mind that is responsible for mental imagery.

14 Look Inside

Language focus: Listening and writing

Level: Intermediate to advanced

Time: 40–50 minutes

Preparation: Bring in a CD player.
Make one copy for each student of the handout with the song and of the treasure chest.
For the variation, a copy for each group of the full song, cut up into its separate lines.

in class

1. Play the song, asking students to try to imagine as vividly as possible what they hear. After they have listened freely, give them each a photocopy with the song lyrics to try to fill in the gaps. Play the song again so they can check their answers.

Look Inside
Chorus:
I want to _____ with you
A treasure chest of things.
I brought it _____
With all the life it brings.
Open it now, look inside
Find all the _____ there,
Open it now, look inside
_____ the images inside.

See a golden summer _____,
See a _____ in the sky.
Gentle waves upon _____
And a blue–green butterfly.
_____ running through a meadow.
Children flying dragon _____.
Dancers circling to the music.
Bright _____ twinkling in the night.

_____ the sound of church bells ringing
Feel a nice cool _____ stream.
Smell a bunch of bright red roses
Then taste _____ with cream.
See a special _____ to go.
A place you're happy and you're _____.
Find a smile and hands to help you
Find a _____ of harmony.

2. Next, students are going to write down what to put in their treasure chest. They decide if what they put in the chest will be for themselves or for someone they would like to give it to as a special present. Keeping the recipient of the treasure chest in mind, they write down what they want to include in it. When they finish, they can read their contents to the class or you can collect the lists to put up on the walls for students to walk around and read.

THE TREASURE CHEST

For _____

_____

_____

_____

_____

_____

_____

_____

_____

By

Variation

As an alternative to the listening gap–fill exercise at the beginning, print out one copy of the song on the next page for each 4 students and cut it up with one line on each strip of paper. In groups of 4, students are given the song lines scrambled. Tell them that the lines of the chorus are underlined, the first verse is written in italics and the second verse in bold. First they try to order them in their groups and then they listen to the song to check. Play the song once more and ask them to listen to the things in the treasure chest and decide which line they like best and tell the rest of their group why.

14 Look Inside

I want to share with you
A treasure chest of things.
I brought it just for you
With all the life it brings.
Open it now, look inside,
Find all the beauty there.
Open it now, look inside,
Enjoy the images inside.

See a golden summer sunset,
See a rainbow in the sky,
Gentle waves upon a warm beach
And a blue-green butterfly.
Horses running through a meadow.
Children flying dragon kites.
Dancers circling to the music.
Bright stars twinkling in the night.

Hear the sound of church bells ringing,
Feel a nice cool mountain stream.
Smell a bunch of bright red roses,
Then taste strawberries with cream.
See a special place to go
A place you're happy and you're free.
Find a smile and hands to help you,
Find a world of harmony.

SECTION 2
LANGUAGE IN MIND

15

Doubling a Picture

Language focus: Question forms

Level: Elementary to advanced

Time: 30–40 minutes

Preparation: Select a large, (at least A3) picture of a person. The picture is best when it has some ambiguity and mystery.

1. Place the picture where all the students can see the person portrayed. Set a chair next to or under the portrait.

2. Go to the back of the room and have a long look at the person. In a low, gentle voice, put these questions to the person portrayed.

   Are you feeling comfortable?
   How old are you?
   What are you thinking?
   How rich / poor are you?
   What kind of father did / do you have?
   What sort of person is attracted to you?
   What kind of parent would you make?
   How do you feel about life?
   And how about death?
   Do I like you?
   Do I fear you?
   Do you leave me indifferent?

3. Suggest the students forget your questions, and write 6–8 questions of their own addressed to the person portrayed. They work individually.

4. Now ask for a volunteer to sit on the chair near the picture and provide the person portrayed with a voice.

5. The students ask their questions and the 'voice' answers them, quickly building up a sense of the person. The students may think of new questions to ask as the characterisation develops.

6. After a while, ask if another student would like to be the 'voice' and repeat the picture interview. Normally the new student builds a new characterisation.

Acknowledgement
We have learnt doubling activities from Bernard Dufeu, author of *Teaching Myself*, OUP 1994, and from John Morgan.

16 Learning a Word with its Family and Friends

Language focus: Working with a network of words

Level: Intermediate to upper Intermediate

Time: 40-50 minutes

Preparation: Bring a large envelope to class.

in class

1. Dictate these words and phrases:

   *mother   to mother somebody   motherly   motherhood
   motherless   to treat your mother right   Mother Russia   mother speak
   the mother of all wars   expectant mother   mother and baby
   a working mother   great grandmother   mother superior
   mother nature   mother country   mother-in-law
   a surrogate mother   a nursing mother   Mother Earth*

2. Ask the students which words or phrases they are not sure about. As far as possible, get students to help each other with meanings. You can explain any that no one knows.

3. Tell the students that you would like them to relax. To help them, count backwards from 15 in a slow rhythmical way, inviting them to close their eyes.

4. Now ask them to get mental images and feelings for the following phrases, pausing for 10 seconds after each:

   *a young mother
   a mother duck
   mother of seven children
   mother and child
   a mother goddess
   grandmother
   the Queen Mother
   a mother-to-be
   to treat your mother right
   a working mother
   necessity is the mother of invention
   don't you mother me!
   mother nature*

5. Ask the students to come back to the classroom, to take pen and paper and to write down the phrases that brought them the most vivid sounds, feelings and images. Compare with a partner, and discuss what they imagined.

6. Then ask them to write a letter to themselves, to be read in one week's time, about the images they had. Tell them that no one else will see these texts. Have them put their letters in the large envelope and staple it shut. A week or two later, you open the envelope in class and give the letters back to their owners.

Note

You can create an activity like this very easily about any words or phrases you want the students to mull over by using an up-to-date corpus-based dictionary and by internet-searching the word to be used. Supposing you have a unit in your book on slavery; you might want students to think deeply about the concept 'slave' and so you could use a guided visualisation like the above on phrases that pivot around 'slave'.

Acknowledgement

The thinking behind this activity comes from Michael Hoey's book *Lexical Priming*, Routledge, 2005.

Elesnakes and Zebradiles

Language focus: Lexical area of animals and their habitats

Level: Lower intermediate to advanced

Time: 25–35 minutes

Preparation: If you wish, computer projection of animals or printed copy.

in class

1. Pre-teach any words for animals and their habitat that are needed for the language level of your class.

2. Ask your students to relax. Say in a quiet, calm voice:

   I'd like you to imagine that you can see in front of you a very friendly dog. See how it wags its tail. Notice its colour, and its size. Start stroking it ... what does its coat feel like?

   Now imagine that the back end of the animal stays a dog, but the front part becomes a cat. See this new animal running around, playing with a ball. Notice how the fur of the front and the back ends joins together. And now change the back of the animal into a zebra.

   Now keep changing the animal. Keep the back end a zebra, and change the front into a crocodile.

   Change the animal again and again. Create as many new animals as you like.

   Pause for 2 or 3 minutes.

   Now choose one of the animals you have created. Choose the one you like best. Give your creature a name. Now, notice its surroundings. It may live in a forest, a desert, a meadow or under water. Watch the animal as it gets some food. Notice how it eats.

   Notice if there are any other animals around like the one you've created. Are they smaller or bigger, or are they the same size? Does your animal live in groups, or does it live alone, or with another animal?

   Notice how your animal interacts with the environment. Try to understand its eating and sleeping habits. What is its relationship with other animals? Where does it live? Where does it sleep? What does it eat? How does it behave?

17 Elesnakes and Zebradiles

*Slowly open your eyes and make notes about what you have found
out about the animal. Then write a text about it. You may want to
add a drawing to your text.*

3. If your students express difficulty seeing the invented animals,
show them the picture on the CD by using a computer projector.

Acknowledgement

The idea for this activity comes from Laura Ellison, *Seeing with Magic
Glasses: A Teacher's View from the Front Line of the Learning
Revolution.* Periklis Pagratis and Great Ocean Publishers, 1993,
p. 124

18 Pronouns and the Reality they Refer to

Language focus:	Deepening students' feel for the English pronoun system
Level:	Elementary to advanced
Time:	30–40 minutes
Preparation:	None.

in class

1. Ask each student to take a piece of paper and write *I* and *ME* in the centre of the page.

2. Dictate these pronouns, and ask the students to write them down on the page where they seem appropriate in relation to *I* and *ME*:

You	*We*	*Each other*
It	*Them*	*He*
We	*She*	*Myself*
Somebody	*One*	*Us*

3. Group the students in fours to compare and explain their placings of the pronouns.

4. Ask the students to sit comfortably and close their eyes if they wish.

5. Tell them you are going to say pronouns to them and you want them to allow the people the pronoun evokes to drift across their mental screens. Pause for 5 to10 seconds between each:

She	*Myself*
Us and them	*Me and you*
Somebody	*They*
Us	*Mine*
Him	*You and me.*
Her and him	

6. In pairs, students choose three of the pronouns or pronoun pairs they heard, and write 4-6 phrases or short sentences using the pronouns or words related to them, organising the phrases or sentences to form a poem. Then they create an interesting way to read their poem to the class (reading in echo; or saying some lines very quietly, others more loudly, etc.).

7. You might want to try having the class stand in a circle with the pair stepping into the centre when they perform their poem.

Example:
You and me
Not three
Not we
Almost us
Why not us?

Variation
Give the students 10 minutes to write down whatever they want about the experience. What they write will be private.

Acknowledgement
The germ of this exercise comes from John Morgan, author of *Vocabulary*, OUP, 2004.

19

Floating Translation

Language focus: To allow meaning to flow from one language into the other

Level: Intermediate to advanced

Time: 50-60 minutes

Preparation: Copy the poem below, one per student.

in class

1. Explain to the students that in the USA one of the street names for cocaine is White Lady.

2. Ask the students to sit comfortably and close their eyes.
Notice your breathing ....
Breathe in ... and think about what you have just been doing ...
Breathe out, and let what you have been doing flow out with your breath ...
Breathe in, and think about last week ...
Breathe out, and let go of last week ...
Breathe in, and think about a worry ...
Breathe out, and let the worry go ...
Listen now to this poem by a black American mother ... Just listen and relax ...

3. Read the poem slowly, with pauses between the lines of about three beats:

White Lady
wants my son
wants my niece
wants Josie's daughter
holds them hard
and close as slavery
what will it cost
to keep our children
what will it cost to buy them back?

White Lady
says I want you
whispers
let me be your lover
whispers
run me through your fingers
feel me
smell me

taste me
love me
nobody understands you like white lady

White Lady
you have chained our sons
in the basement
of the big house
white lady
you have walked our daughters
out into the streets
white lady
what do we have to pay
to repossess our children
white lady
what do we have to owe
to own our own at last?

Now I will read the poem to you again, and this time let the English words become mother-tongue words in your mind ... As you listen to the sounds, allow the words from your language to take their place ... If you don't find a word in your own language, keep the English word ...

This time, leave a count of five between the lines.

4. After this second reading, bring the students gently back and ask them to work on their own, writing down a mixture of the English and L1 words and phrases that come back to them. Allow 5 minutes for this.

5. Give them the text, and ask them to work together in pairs to produce a full L1 rendering. (If your class is multi-mother tongue, then pair same–L1 students. If there is anyone without a partner, they can work alone on their translation.) Go round helping with the language.

6. Now put the students into groups of three. They listen to each other's translations. (In multi-mother-tongue groups this can be an interesting musical experience.)

7. Round off the class with a short discussion of how they feel about this mother's lamenting cocaine as a child-thief.

Variation
You can use any text of your choice, though for this exercise the utterances need to be relatively short. Once the students are used to the transposition of thoughts into mother tongue from English, try it the other way round.

Note
For more L1– L2 activities see *Using Mother Tongue*, Sheelagh Deller et al, Delta Publishing, 2002.

Acknowledgement
The poem, by Lucille Clifton, is from *Blessing the Boats*, BOA Editions, 2000.

20 The Present Perfect in Images

Language focus: The present perfect tense

Level: Elementary to advanced

Time: 30–40 minutes

Preparation: A copy of the text for each student.

in class

1. Ask the students to sit comfortably and to close their eyes if they wish. Tell them to remember the following, giving them enough time after each to imagine the things suggested.

   Three things I have done today that I am happy with ...
   Three things I have done this week that I am happy with ...
   Three things I have done this year that I am happy with ...

   Two things I have not yet done today ...
   Two things I have not yet done this week ...
   Two things that I have not yet done this year ...

   One thing I have learnt today ...
   One thing I have learnt this week ...
   One thing I have learnt this year ...

   How does today feel, so far?
   How does this week feel, so far?
   How does this year feel, so far?

2. Bring the students back from their thoughts.

3. Give each person the text you read, and ask them to write down whatever it was that came to mind during the visualisation, stopping after *One thing I've learnt this year ...* Ask them to use the present perfect tense when appropriate.

4. Go round and help with the language.

5. Pair the students and let them read each other's sentences, and then discuss the last three questions.

6. Round off the lesson with this joke on the board:
   Politician: You've lived on this farm for 80 years ... have you had a good life?
   Farmer: Dunno yet!

21 Revising Vocabulary using Imagery

Language focus: Vocabulary review.

Level: Elementary to advanced

Time: 15–20 minutes

Preparation: None.

1. Ask the students to scan back over the past two or three units of the course book and pick 5–6 words they find hard to commit to memory.

2. Each student chooses two of these words to put on the board.

3. Help with the meanings of any words someone doesn't know

4. Ask the students to shut their eyes and notice their breathing.

5. Slowly and loudly say one of the more concrete words on the board.

6. Ask the students to open their eyes, and then ask four or five people what they heard, felt or saw when you said the word. Ask them to be specific about their images.

7. Repeat the above procedure with 8–12 more words from those on the board, including some abstract ones.

8. Discuss with the students whether they feel the words will be easier to remember now. Suggest they try creating images of words when they are revising on their own.

22 Flipping a Picture Over

Language focus: Revision of vocabulary

Level: Elementary to advanced

Time: 5–10 minutes

Preparation: Draw pictures for words you want to revise on a piece of cardboard big enough for your students to be able to discern the pictures clearly, or find an appropriate photo in a magazine and stick it onto a piece of cardboard.

in class

1. Stand in front of your class, holding the picture, with its back to the students, between two fingers of each hand so you can easily flip it around.

2. Tell your students to pay attention as you will show them a picture for just a very short time, then want them to call out words. Flip the picture around so that the students can only see it for a second at most, then flip it back again. Wait for the students to call out some words.

3. Flip the picture again several times, each time eliciting more words from the students.

4. When the students have named all the words, show them the picture for one minute and ask them to remember as many details as possible.

5. After the minute, ask them to close their eyes. Ask detailed questions about the picture (e.g. *What's the woman standing next to the tree wearing?*), and get your students to answer with their eyes still closed.

Variation
Alternatively, and depending also on the words you want to revise, write a set of words, in different colours, on your piece of cardboard. The questions in the last phase then would be something along the lines of '*What colour is the word ...?*'

Note
This activity has a very positive effect on the students' ability to focus their attention. Used regularly, it is a good means of developing students' visual memory skills well.

Rotating Sentences in your Mind

Language focus: Experimenting with word order

Level: Elementary to advanced

Time: 20–30 minutes

Preparation: None.

in class

1. Write up on the board: *Never on Sunday.*

2. Ask each student to copy the phrase, but moving the first word to the end of the utterance: *On Sunday, never!*

3. Now ask the students to each move the first word into third position: *Sunday? Never on!*

4. Ask the students if they see meaning in the new utterance. ('On Sunday? There's never a film on a Sunday.')

5. Now ask the students to sit comfortably and shut their eyes.

6. Tell them you are going to give them a four-word sentence (*This is not London.*) and ask them to mentally move the first word on the left one space to the right (they should have *Is this not London?*), and then to decide if the new utterance is meaningful.

7. They then mentally take the new sentence and move the original first word one more space to the right (*Is not this London?*) and check if the new sentence is meaningful ... they go on till they get back to the original: *This is not London.*

8. When the group has finished their internal language work ask them to work individually and write down the three new utterances. Ask them to add words to the left or right to fully bring out their meaning, eg: *Is not London this* could become *Is not London this, this hive of seething humanity?*

9. Have the students move around and: read each other's sentences to see if they can find someone with three sentences similar to their own.

Variation
Here are two more snatches of speech that work for this activity:
    Well, yes and no.   *Yes, I think so.*

Acknowledgement
We learnt to mentally rotate sentences from Adrian Underhill.

24

A Recipe

Language focus: Lexical area of cooking and the kitchen

Level: Intermediate to advanced

Time: 30–40 minutes

Preparation: None.
For the variation, bring flour, a rolling pin, a sieve, a bottle of oil to class.

in class

1. Write the word *cooking* in the middle of the board and ask students to come up silently and surround it with the words that they associate with this idea. Tell them to write in English if they can, and in their L1 if not.

2. If they haven't suggested *bowl, dough, rolling pin, frying pan* and *sieve*, add these and explain what they are. Help the students to turn all the words on the board into English.

3. Ask them to relax, close their eyes and think of a kitchen they know. Ask them:
   Which parts of the kitchen are light and which are dark?
   How many colours can you see in this kitchen?
   As you stand in the kitchen, what sounds can you hear?
   How hot or cold is it here?
   Where are the mixing bowls kept?
   And the flour?

4. Tell them to do these things mentally in their imaginary kitchen:

   Get a packet of flour ...
   Take a sieve and a bowl ...
   Sieve half the flour into the bowl ...
   Boil some water ...
   Pour a little of the boiling water onto the flour ...
   Mix the flour and water ...
   Leave the dough to stand for 15 minutes ...
   Take a rolling pin and roll a small piece of dough flat ...
   Roll it thin ...
   Drip a couple of drops of oil into it ...
   Do this several times till you finish the dough ...
   Heat up a frying pan ...
   Put the leaves of dough into it ...
   Turn the leaves of dough over ...
   Take them out of the pan and roll them round bits of roast duck, spring onion and cucumber ...
   You have just prepared Peking Duck! Try it, if you would like to.

5. Group the students in fours to describe to each other how the 'cooking' went for each of them. Ask the foursomes to write up the recipe collaboratively.

6. If you wish, for homework for the next class, ask students to come with a favourite recipe of theirs, a simple one. In pairs, each student does their *cooking* guided visualisation

Variation
Begin the class in the following way:

1. Show the class your kitchen equipment.

2. Sieve some flour.

3. Add water to the flour to make the word *dough* clear.

4. Demonstrate rolling dough flat.

5. Drip drops of oil onto the dough …

Note
We have chosen the recipe for Mongolian pancakes as they are central to a classical dish in world-renowned northern Chinese cuisine. If you prefer, you can do this activity with any other recipe you think your students might find interesting.

25 Dreamy Listening

Language focus: To help the students understand different modes of listening

Level: Intermediate to advanced

Time: 50-60 minutes

Preparation: The day before, tell the students to think of a 2- or 3-minute story to tell in the next class.

in class

1. Group the students into fours. Ask them to decide who is A, who is B, C and D.

2. Tell them the A students will be the first to tell their stories. Tell the B students they are to listen and take written notes of any language mistakes they notice *and* of all the excellent things A says. Tell the C students to listen to the story and try to see the story in images, letting their minds drift off happily if anything the storyteller says invites them into their own world of experience. Tell them to dreamily enjoy leaving the story, and then maybe coming back in. Tell the D students to pay full attention to the story, as they will have to say it back to the teller at the end of the telling. They will retell it as if they were the teller.

3. The As tell their stories.

4. The Ds then repeat back the story they have just heard to the As.

5. The Bs refer to their notes and tell the As some of the good and less good language they used.

6. Finally the Cs give an account of what happened in their dreamy listening.

7. Do the activity three more times, rotating roles so that everybody has been in all four roles.

8. Round off the class with a general discussion on listening modes.

Dreamy Listening

Note

There are many other listening roles beyond those outlined above. Some of these are to listen:

a) only for keywords, associating them with your own life.

b) musically, focusing on speed of utterance, pitch (high/low), and volume.

c) watching which gestures go with which words: consciously following the rhythm of the hands, face and upper body, and of the speaker's breathing.

d) for all the words and phrases that make you feel happy.

26 Visual Error Correction

Language focus: Correcting errors in a discreet but memorable way

Level: Elementary to advanced

Time: A few minutes whenever working on a specific error

Preparation: Have ready some sets of coloured paper or card, about 10 × 10 cm (6" × 6"), two each of the same colour; plus a thick highlighter or marker pen.

in class

1. In a free-speaking phase of the lesson, when a student makes an error you decide is in some way typical of errors your class habitually make in a certain language area, take a piece of the coloured paper and draw a symbol or write a letter of the word so that it's clearly visible, in order to use it as a visual anchor to remind the students not to make this error.

2. If you pick, say, omission of the third-person-singular *s*, write a large S on the card. Stick this up on the wall so your students can easily see it.

3. Ask the student to repeat the sentence. When you hear the mistake, simply point at the sign, and smile at the student. Wait for the student to correct their error, or if needed, whisper the correct form for the student and get them to repeat the sentence after you.

4. The next time the same error occurs, follow the same pattern. Stop the student, point at the sign on the wall, smile, and wait for the student to self-correct their utterance.

5. Proceed like this for some time. Then take the card off the wall.

6. The next time the same error occurs, take a card of the same colour, don't write anything on it, and stick it on the same spot on the wall where the previous card had been. Wait for the student to self-correct their error.

7. Carry on like this for some time, then take the card off. When the same error occurs after some time, it is usually enough to point at the same spot on the wall (where there is now no card any more). *And remember to smile!*

Note

Error correction needs to be handled extremely sensitively, because there is always the danger that students will misunderstand the teacher's correction of an error and consequently create negative beliefs about their own language-learning capabilities (*I'm hopeless at this. I'll never get this right.* etc.)

This activity is very useful in avoiding this problem, since it sorts out the message from the meta-message. The message to the student is that there is something wrong about their sentence, whereas the meta-message (the teacher's friendly smile) is clearly saying, *You're okay! – it's just the sentence created that needs a little correction.*

What have I Learnt Today?

Language focus: Lesson review

Level: Lower intermediate to advanced

Time: 5–10 minutes

Preparation: None.

1. At the end of a lesson, when there are only a few minutes left, ask your students to get into a comfortable sitting position. In a calm, quiet voice, say:

   I'd like you to close your eyes and take a few minutes to go back over the lesson. Remember the moment you entered the classroom today. What expectations did you have? How were you feeling? When you go through the different phases of the lesson in your mind now, what strong memories do you have about it? What was especially important for you? What was especially useful?
   Now think of what you did during the lesson. In which part or parts of the lesson were you most active? What did you do then? Did you work on your own, or collaborate with others?
   Now think of what you learnt in this lesson. What new words did you learn? What phrases? Any constructions? Did you gain any new insights into the English language?
   How will you make sure that you will remember what you learnt today? Did you get any homework? If so, when will you do it? Are you going to do any revision work based on what you learnt today? Now imagine a future situation in real life where you will be able to use what you have learnt today. See, hear and feel yourself using the new language confidently with other people. What do you still need to learn so that you can use English even more successfully? Take a minute to complete this, and then come back to the classroom.

2. Write the following stem sentences on the board and invite students to complete them, speaking aloud:

   In today's lesson I learnt ...
   The most important phase in the lesson for me was when ...
   I enjoyed ... most.
   I'd like to learn more about ...

   Variation
   The basic format of this visualisation can be used as a basis for evaluation of a learning period longer than a lesson (i.e. a week, month, term or school year).

The Irregular-Verbs Gym

Language focus: Memorising irregular verb forms

Level: Elementary to advanced

Time: 5 minutes

Preparation: Select a list of irregular verbs you want your students to remember.

1. Ask your students to stand up and watch you. When they are attentive, say the first form of an irregular verb that has all three different forms, carrying out a specific movement at the same time. Then say the past form, make a different movement, and finally say the past participle, again making another – again different – movement. For example:

Say	Do
write	*stretch out your arms high above your head*
wrote	*touch your knees*
written	*touch your toes*

2. Ask your students to say the forms and carry out the actions with you. Then ask them to work through another irregular verb in the same way (again, select one where the three forms are different from one another, e.g. *swim*).

3. Then select an irregular verb where past and past participle forms are the same, e.g. *find*, and ask your students to work through it. Many students will repeat the three different movements, but you should get them to make an identical movement for *found* (past) and *found* (past participle) instead.

4. Then get them to do an irregular verb where all three forms are the same, e.g. *put*; they will need to make only a single movement.

5. Carry on practising with all the irregular verbs you want your students to consolidate.

6. The next time you do the same activity, your students will be making three different movements the first time (because you will have named an irregular verb with three different forms), so praise them and say YES, holding up three fingers as a visual anchor. Do the same with two fingers (for a verb with two different forms) and one finger for a verb whose three forms are all the same. These finger signs will further help students to remember the irregular verb forms.

28 The Irregular-Verbs Gym

Note
This activity too starts from a kinaesthetic learning experience, and gradually leads over to the students' visual memory.

Acknowledgement
We learnt this activity from Gertrude Wissiol, a teacher in Munich.

29 Getting Ready for Reading

Language focus: Activating previous knowledge before reading

Level: Intermediate to advanced

Time: 40–50 minutes

Preparation: Slide on computer projector, or printed for students to see. One copy of reading text (overleaf) for each student

1. Ask students to get an image in their mind of the earth – they may want to see it as if they were looking down from a space ship, they may want to focus on a particular part, or they may just experience a feeling about it.

2. Show students the picture below and ask them to look at it for a moment and to write down in one sentence what they think the artist is trying to say.

3. Have them check to see if the person next to them has written something similar. Call on several students to read their sentences. If the class is not too large, you could also go around the room and have each student say their sentence.

4. Brainstorm the problems they can think of that human beings are creating for the planet. If they need to, they can express some ideas in their mother tongue and you can help to translate into English. Write their suggestions on the board, and as you write ask them to bring up images in their mind associated with each. Then tell them they are going to read a transcript of a conversation where several concerned professionals are talking about the environment.

5. After reading the conversation, each student will choose one of the environmental professionals (Ann, Mike ...) and in pairs they will prepare a short role-play continuing the discussion and adding some of their own ideas about the topic. They then perform their role-plays for the class.

Several experts on the environment are discussing some of the main issues:

Ann: Everywhere we look the planet is saying 'Enough!' If we don't start thinking of the future of the world instead of being concerned only with our immediate wishes, there may not even be a future. There is no doubt that human beings are the most destructive species that exists.

Mike: I hate to have to agree with you, because that is a very black view of the future – but unfortunately there are many indications that this may be the world we are creating for our children or our grandchildren. We see this in the air, on land and in the sea. The ice cap melting at the North Pole has been greatly reduced, thousands of square kilometres of forest are lost every year, and rainfall is declining in many areas, bringing deserts and famine for millions of people. Do you want to hear more?

Sylvia: Not really. And I wish it weren't true, but nature is constantly sending us warnings that all is not well. When we stop to think about the reasons for the situation, we inevitably come to one fact: selfishness and greed predominate. We only think of consuming more and more, having more money and more possessions, as if this would make us happy. In the process we are losing our values and creating disaster for the earth.

Danny: There have always been climatic changes – some rather spectacular – but never has there been such rapid change. Things have gone totally out of control. What used to take thousands of years now happens in one hundred years. And there is no doubt that human beings are responsible. We have to realise that there are values, there are responsibilities that are more important than buying bigger cars, or industry making enormous profits.

Amy: I agree with everything you've said, but I am hopeful. More and more people are becoming aware of their duty towards the planet – you know, turning off lights you don't need, using public transport or bikes, using clean energy sources. For me it is especially important to teach children to care for their world. I remember when I was about 10 years old, I saw a film at school about how we have to take care of our water resources – that must have really influenced me because now many years later I am really concerned about saving water.

Joel: Yes, that is important, and the little bit you save and the little bit I save adds up. But without the cooperation of industry and of governmental agencies, I doubt we can win the battle. The first-world countries enjoy a high material standard of living, but at what cost? Governments need to join with industry to ensure no ecological crimes go unpunished. After all, even the leaders of the most powerful countries and the wealthiest companies cannot wish to leave their children and grandchildren a world unfit to live in. It is time we all listened to what our planet is saying, and act on it.

30 Images to Poem

Language focus:	Collaborative writing
Level:	Lower intermediate to advanced
Time:	40 minutes
Preparation:	For the variation, OHP with some blank transparencies and permanent markers.

in class

1. Brainstorm with the whole class a list of values – *freedom*, *peace*, *tolerance* etc. This may be easier if they have already done Activity 72, Positive Qualities. Write the values on the board.

2. Divide the students into groups of four. Each group chooses one of the values as the title to the poem they are going to write as a group. They all think of the value, and try to get several different images in mind that somehow they associate with the value chosen. Get each student to cut or tear four strips of paper, and on each strip write down a sentence or a phrase describing one of the images. Make it clear that an image may be in any sensory mode including felt images. (For example, if *Peace* were chosen, students might write: *A white dove flying in the sky* or *Feeling love for all the world*.)

3. The group will then have 16 lines for their poem. They decide on eight, two from each person in the group, arranging them in any way they wish and adding a few words if necessary to complete the poem. Each group then decides how they want to read the poem to the rest of the class. Some possibilities you can suggest: each person reads two lines, they all read together, one reads and the others mime the poem, they read without the title and the class has to guess the title, etc.

Variation
Alternatively, they can write the poem on an OHP transparency and include a drawing to project as they read it aloud.

Acknowledgement
We saw this activity done by Grethe Hooper Hansen. A version of it can be found in Gerngross, Günter and Puchta *Pictures into Action*, Prentice-Hall, 1992.

31 Speak, Listen and Draw

Language focus: Language of description

Level: Lower intermediate to advanced

Time: 20 minutes

Preparation: Two pictures on computer projector or photos from magazines, one for each student.

in class

1. Pre-teach vocabulary necessary to describe a picture (*in the upper right-hand corner* etc.).

2. In pairs, each student is going to describe a picture. Have students sit so that only A can see the screen. As describes the picture to Bs, who try to imagine it and make a drawing of what they see in the mind's eye. Bs can ask As for more details (*Is it very big? Is it here or more to the left?*) and As can suggest corrections (*It should be closer to the bottom of the picture ...*).

3. Have the Bs turn around and look at the original. Then they reverse roles, and the Bs describe while the As listen and draw.

4. The pictures used may be of a very concrete or a more abstract nature, and if students have colours to use this can make the activity more interesting.

Variation
Make a collection of photos from magazines, one for each student. Give all the students a photo each, but they don't show them to their partner until after they have described them and the partner has completed the drawing. After they have finished, they can exchange their photos and drawings with another pair of students and then talk about the differences between the photos and the drawings done by their classmates.

Picture 1

Picture 2

Cooperative Descriptions

Language focus: Language of description

Level: Elementary to advanced

Time: 30 minutes

Preparation: Provide one envelope for each three students in your class with three pictures of objects, animals, or buildings in each one. Have one or two extra photos.

in class

1. Group students in threes. Give each group an envelope. If you need to have one or two groups with four, add one of the spare photos to the envelopes of those groups. Tell each group not to let the other groups see their photos. Working quietly, so the others don't hear what they say, together the members of each group write a description of each object without naming it, using three or four sentences. They should use the first person to describe the object; for example, if they describe a table they could say *I am brown. I am made of wood. I have four legs. I am used in a dining room.* Move around the room helping with any language needed.

2. When all groups have finished, each student in a group reads one of the descriptions and the other groups try to imagine what is being described, with each sentence completing the picture a little more. This can be done as a game, with students raising their hand to guess when they think they know, and the first group to get the right answer gets two points. They can lose a point if they make a wrong guess.

33 Always Someone to Talk to

Language focus: Inner speaking for language practice

Level: Elementary to advanced

Time: 20 minutes (and for students, some time out of class)

Preparation: None.

in class

1. Remind the class that students sometimes complain that they have no one to practise speaking with, but tell them that they always have one person to talk to – themselves – and that in our own language all of us talk to ourselves sometimes. They can practise a lot by doing the same in English.

2. Ask them to take out a piece of paper. When you ask a question or give them a prompt, they should observe what they say to themselves. You can use the ones below or think of others appropriate for your students. Tell them they can use their mother tongue if they need to, but to try to write as much as they can in English. After each prompt, pause about 10 seconds, then ask them to write down any words they said to themselves in either language, even if what they say is *This is silly* or *I don't want to do this!*

3. You might model first how you talk to yourself. Try this; point to a pile of papers and say: *Have to finish correcting. Just too much. Really tired today. Maybe later. Yeah.* Explain that we talk in short phrases, not long complete sentences.

   Prompts:
   Last weekend … That problem I have … The government … School … This activity … Me … Them … Nice … Life … Fun … Tiger …

4. First, put them in pairs and ask them to share some of their inner speech. Then ask if they want to share with the class anything they both said or anything they found interesting about the activity.

5. Review the importance of developing inner speech in their new language, and recommend further work to be done out of class.

out of class

1. Tell students when they have down time with nothing to do (riding on a bus, waiting for someone …) they can practise and improve their English using inner speech. Either give them a list of several options to choose from or make one suggestion to be done several times during the week. To encourage them to try this exercise you could have them decide on the option

individually and tell them that the following week in pairs they will have to tell their partner which option they used and how it went. Try these or invent some of your own which would be appropriate for your group:

· *Imagine a conversation between two people you see.*

· *At the end of the day, tell yourself what were the most important things that happened.*

· *Imagine a phone conversation with a friend you haven't seen for several weeks.*

· *Think of someone you'd like to say something to, but you don't dare. Do it in inner speech. They won't argue with you!*

· *As you go somewhere on foot or in a bus, train or car, try to describe the things you see.*

· *Try to observe your self–talk during the day, the little comments you make to yourself. When you notice one, translate it into English. If the thought is negative ('I'll never learn this'), translate it first into something more positive ('If I work hard enough, I could learn this') and then into English.*

· *In the evening, plan the following day in English.*

Note

There are many reasons for focusing on inner speech, a type of auditory imaging which puts our thoughts into words. Research has shown that not only is comprehensible input necessary for second-language acquisition, but learners also need to work with new language and express themselves through some form of output. However, they may be afraid of making mistakes in front of their peers and the teacher, and so be unwilling to produce the necessary output. Inner-speech work can give them the opportunity to do so in a totally safe way. While they won't be getting external corrective feedback, they will be motivated to resolve any doubts they have. When they don't have the right word to say what they want, they are likely try to find it as soon as possible in dictionaries or by asking others. With inner speech we are saying what we feel the need to say, and so this results in a much greater interest in having the necessary linguistic material to do so at our disposal.

Inner speech work is a great help, not just for the general learning process but also for when learners have a specific use of language in mind. They can rehearse answering possible questions for an oral exam or interacting with someone about a certain topic (ordering food in a restaurant, asking someone directions ...). Perhaps one of the best tests for successful acquisition of a language is when you begin to speak to yourself naturally in the language!

Acknowledgements

This activity owes a lot to Tomlinson and Avila (2007a), and to Marc Helgesen's practical use of inner voice principles ('Talk to Yourself', *English Teaching Professional*, October 2003).

Automatic Writing

Language focus: Generating ideas for writing

Level: Lower intermediate to advanced

Time: 15–20 minutes, and 5–10 minutes a week later

Preparation: Bring in a large envelope for Lesson 1.

in class

Lesson 1

1. In a gentle voice, ask your class to do the following:

   While you are sitting, press your feet firmly against the ground. Do so for six seconds, then relax.

   Stand up. Keep your knees straight. Stretch your arms as high up into the air as you can. Hold it for six seconds, then relax again. Sit down.

   Make very tight fists. Hold them for six seconds, then let go.

   Pull up your shoulders as high as you can. Hold them up for six seconds, then let them drop down again.

   Tighten your face muscles. Grimace for six seconds, then relax.

   Now close your eyes. Breathe slowly and regularly. Imagine that whenever you breathe out, a little of the stress and the tension you have within you disappears, and whenever you breathe in, you take in new and fresh energy. Imagine that you breathe this energy into your body, especially wherever you might still feel a bit tense. Take 1 or 2 minutes to enjoy that.

2. Tell your students to get pen and paper and do non–stop writing for 5 minutes. Tell them that nobody but themselves will see what they write. Encourage them not to judge in any way whatever text they produce, but just allow automatic writing to take place, and jot down whatever comes to mind. If worrying thoughts about their writing come to mind, they should write them down too, but not allow those thoughts to interrupt the flow of their writing.

3. When students have finished, ask them to put their texts into a large envelope, and staple it shut. Tell them they will get them back the following week.

Lesson 2

1. A week later, open the envelope in class and hand out the texts for the students to read. Get them to comment on the writing process and their feelings about the texts they produced (remind them, though, that they don't have to reveal what they actually wrote).

Notes

This relaxation activity is excellent if your class is tired when your lesson starts. It helps to release tension, and while your students are concentrating on the movements they will notice that they slowly start to relax. You will also notice a change in your students' attention and state of concentration.

Especially with the grimacing bit, you are guaranteed to get laughter from your class. This is nothing to worry about – quite the opposite, as laughter has a relaxing effect. Allow for it, and enjoy it too.

Acknowledgement

The writing activity is based on an idea in Henriette A. Klauser, *Writing on Both Sides of the Brain: Breakthrough Techniques for People Who Write.* Harper Collins, 1987.

SECTION 3
STORIES STORIES TELL

35 From Listening to Reading to Writing

Language focus:	To help students go from a poem to their own writing
Level:	Intermediate to advanced
Time:	40 minutes
Preparation:	A copy of the poem (in no. 5 below) per student.

in class

1. Tell students:

   Bring to mind an old person you know. How do you feel about them? Imagine what they do during the day. Try to feel what it would be like to be that person.

2. In pairs, the students describe the person to their partner.

3. Ask the students to sit comfortably and close their eyes. Say:

   You are sitting in a café ...
   You are in Egypt ... you are sitting in a café in Alexandria ...
   You hear many voices ... you hear the slap of cards being thrown down on the table ...
   Old men smoke water pipes ... gurgle ... gurgle ... bubble ... bubble ...
   Now I am going to let you hear words and phrases from a poem ... allow the words to flow over you and through you ... If you understand them, that's fine ... If there are words you don't know ... that's fine too.

4. From in front of the class, speak the words that follow, using a deep, slow voice. Make the words resonate. Pause for a beat of three between each of the lines. Here are the words:

   Old ... old man
   With newspaper ... at a table
   Alone ... noise around
   Abject ... in age's fears ....
   Did not enjoy ... the years ....
   Was strong and sound ...
   Understands ... old ... he knows
   Time of youth ... glows
   Short the road ... like yesterday ...
   Trusted Prudence ... absurd
   Lying words ....
   Plenty of time ... ardours restrained ... sacrifice of joy ....
   Vainly wise ....

Mocked by chances gone ...
Thoughts ... memories deep
Dazed ... falls asleep
All alone.

Pause
Now I am going to read you the whole poem, but I am going to do this from the back of the class.

5. Then go round to stand behind the students and read the whole poem, pausing briefly between the lines. Read at a moderate speed:

An old man
An old man with a newspaper
Sits huddled at a table there
Alone with all the noise around.
He thinks abject in age's fears
How little he enjoyed the years
When he was strong and sane and sound.
He understands he's old: he knows,
And yet the time of youth still glows –
How short the road! – like yesterday.
He trusted Prudence – how absurd! –
She tricked him with a lying word:
'Plenty of time. Another day.'
Ardours restrained, the sacrifice
Of joy – to have been vainly wise
Is mocked by every chance that's gone ...
But with his thoughts and memories deep
Presently dazed, he falls asleep
Over the table all alone.

I will read you the poem a second time ...

6. After the second reading, gently bring the students back into the classroom and quietly give out copies of the poem. Ask them to read it silently. They can ask you about any vocabulary they don't understand, but then try to help them guess the general meaning from the context. For example, if they don't know *abject*, ask them if they think it means he feels really happy or really sad.

7. Tell the students they have 20 minutes to write about one of the following:

What I felt as I heard and read the poem.
What was this man like when he was young?
What do I feel about growing old?
An old person I know (a poem, story or description).

8. Put the students into pairs or groups of three or four, and tell them to share what they wrote.

Variation

If your class is used to working more autonomously, have them write freely anything they wish after reading the poem, without putting their name on their writing. Collect their writing and put it up around the room. They then walk around reading each other's work.

Acknowledgement

Poem by C.P. Cavafy, translated by John Mavrogordato, Chatto and Windus, 1951, p. 17.

36 Expanding a Story

Language focus:	Enriching a bare narrative
Level:	Intermediate to advanced
Time:	20–30 minutes
Preparation:	None.

in class

1. Tell your class that as they relax you are going to tell them the bare bones of a story, pausing here and there so they can fill out the story in their own minds.

2. Ask the students to close their eyes and notice their breathing and to imagine they are breathing in energy-giving air. Tell them that as they breathe out, they are getting rid of stress and tension.

3. And now the story:
   Once upon a time there was a town and all the people who lived there were happy.
   They were happy all day and every day.
   I have forgotten what the town looked like and how the people were dressed. I don't remember if it was winter or summer in the story. I don't know what kind of happy their happy was. Please remember what I have forgotten.

   15-second pause
   And these happy townspeople built a wall right round their town. And they built just one gate to go into and out of the town. I don't understand why people who are so happy would want to build a wall right round the place where they lived. Maybe you have an idea why they built that wall.

   15-second pause
   One year exactly after the wall had gone up, a terrible thing happened. This enormous giant, a huge man, came and stood at the one gate to the town. Every time anybody tried to open the gate and leave the town the giant jumped in the air and said, 'Pwwooooh!' The huge noise he made terrified the people. What are your thoughts at this point in the story? You have a moment to enjoy them.

   15-second pause
   And the people in the town began to get hungry because the giant would not let them go out through the gate, and he refused to let people from outside in. There was little food; there was little water.

So the townspeople went to their king and said, 'You are our king – you have to do something about this giant.'
I used to know what sort of man the king was, but it has gone from my mind. Can you help me by getting a real feeling for who this king was?

15–second pause
The king put on his armour and covered his head with his great plumed helmet.
He took his sword in his right hand and left his palace. The king was very much afraid. 'But I am the king,' he said to himself. He walked down the High Street, followed by all his subjects, by the townsfolk. When he reached the gate in the wall, he ordered his men to open it.
The giant saw him coming through the gate. Once the king was right outside the gate, the giant leapt in the air and went 'Pwooooh!' very loudly. It sounded like thunder. The earth shook. The king did not move. He just stood there. He did not move back.
The huge giant began to get smaller. He shrank and he shrank until he was the same size as the king. But he went on shrinking until he was only about 6 inches tall.
The king put out his hand and picked the little giant up.
'What is your name?' the king asked.
'Fear,' the midget giant said … and the king set him down so he could run away into the long grass outside the town walls.

4. Ask the students to come back to the classroom and form groups of three to discuss the following: *What was the town like? Why was the wall built? What was the king like?* They should then try to agree on the meaning of the story.

5. Round off with feedback on the activity.

Acknowledgements
We learnt this 'sandwich storytelling' from John Morgan's *Once Upon a Time*, CUP, 1986.
We first heard the *Happy People* story told by Robert MacCall, of Hamburg, Germany.

37 From Sounds to Mumblings to Stories

Language focus: To help students to develop a skeletal text into a rich one

Level: Elementary to advanced

Time: 40–50 minutes

Preparation: Prepare a sequence of sounds or use the one on the CD
Bring in a CD player

in class

1. Explain to the students that they will shortly hear a series of sounds and that their task is to imagine the story that the sounds begin to tell. Explain to them that once the sound sequence is over, they should start mumbling, or whispering, to themselves the story they imagine. The sounds will only be part of the story they invent. Tell them that they will mumble the story twice. The first time they mumble, they may be short of words they want, and they may make plenty of mistakes. The second time they will try to enrich it and eliminate as many mistakes as they can.

2. Ask the class to sit comfortably and close their eyes. Then play the CD.

   Noises that will be heard:
   Three deep sighs with a pause between each.
   A faint wailing sound that gradually gets stronger and stronger.
   Someone walking, limping slowly and loudly.
   A tapping softly on a door three times.
   A knocking on the door four times.
   A kicking at the door five times.
   Sound of the door opening ... pause ...
   A long scream dying away slowly.
   Sounds of running feet.
   A loud shout.

3. Tell the students: *This is the end of the sound sequence ... Please now start thinking about the story you imagine ... you will have several minutes to mumble it twice ...*

4. Allow 3–5 minutes. Then ask students to work on their own and write a one-page version of their story. Tell them they have 15 minutes for this. Go round supplying language they need.

5. Group them in fours, and they each read their story to their group.

Variations

1. If learners share their mother tongue, after they have written the first version, you can play the sound sequence again and have them write a second story in their mother tongue, without reference to the English one. In groups of three they each read both versions.
2. If the class is very low level, the introduction can be given in L1.

Notes

We feel that this is not just a one-off exercise; the more students do this kind of work, the better they get at it.

If students have equipment for making a tape, they can make further sound sequences to be used in class. In her book *Lessons from the Learners* Sheelagh Deller (Pilgrims Longman, 1990) rightly affirms that teachers themselves do more preparation work than is necessary. And students find it very confidence-building to see that they can produce material for classroom use.

Acknowledgement

The idea of using sound sequences as a story-making trigger comes from Alan Maley and Alan Duff, *Sounds Intriguing*, CUP, 1979.
We owe the mumbling technique to Anne Pechou.

38 Creating a Story

Language focus:	Creative writing
Level:	Intermediate to advanced
Time:	40–50 minutes
Preparation:	Optional: computer projection of paintings or printed copy. Bring in a CD player.

in class

1. Write the following words on the board and ask your students to look at them and to imagine a story in which the words and expressions might appear. Help them with the meaning of any words they don't know.

gas mask	*factory*
skyline	*menacing*
sunrise	*pill*
destruction	*energy drink*

2. In pairs, have them tell each other in one or two sentences what story they have imagined.

3. Tell students the following story and ask them to try to see it as a film playing in their mind:

   Areta woke up early. Alex wasn't in bed but she knew that he was probably reading as usual. She escaped from the inhuman world around her by listening to music, and he did so by reading. She had washed their protective suits the night before and so they were as white as snow. How long would they stay that way once they stepped out the door of their building and into the air which smelled of destruction? She dressed quickly and took her food pill with a glass of Formula 21 energy drink and gave Alex his. Breakfast over, she told him to dress quickly as they shouldn't get to the factory late. They put on their new gas masks in preparation for leaving for work. Never in a hurry and never worried about the dangers of life facing them, he sat down again, put his feet up and finished reading a story, while she looked out the window at the city skyline. The sunrise painted the sky pink and blue above the cold, impersonal city. In the horror she saw before her there was a strange, menacing beauty.

4. Individually, students write three sentences stating things that were the same or that were different in the first and second stories. (*In story 1, I imagined a lot of people, and in story 2 there were only two. In both stories I saw a city at sunrise.*)

5. Students look at the illustrations and, listening to music, imagine how the story might end. Individually, they write an ending for the story and then read it to their partner.

Variations
If the level of the group is lower, they can be given the text to read as you tell them the story.

Picture 1

Picture 2

39 Dreaming your Way into a Story's Vocabulary

Language focus: Understanding a few words, understanding more words, understanding a whole story

Level: Elementary to lower intermediate

Time: 20–30 minutes

Preparation: Optional: bring in a CD player. Write the bones of the story below on photocopies, or on an OHP transparency, or have it ready in your computer to project it for the class.
Prepare to tell the story below in your own special way.

in class

1. For lower levels, in order to ensure they know the essential vocabulary, put the following on the board for them to match the definition to the word:

donkey	person who grows food
well	grey animal used for work
farmer	place in the ground to get water.

2. Tell the students, in their L1, that they are going to hear some words and phrases from a story and that they will understand some words, and half-understand others – and some they may not understand at all.

3. Ask them to lay their heads on the desk and shut their eyes. Tell them to notice their breathing. Then either play CD track no. 6 or tell them this skeleton story, leaving 5–10 seconds between each of the phrases:

A farmer, a farmer in Italy, a farmer in Italy
a donkey, a donkey ... the farmer has a donkey
water ... water in a well, in a well ... water in a well
no water in the well ... no water ... the well is dry
donkey in the well, no water ... donkey in the well
farmer thinks: 'donkey is old ' 'donkey is very old'... 'donkey no good'
farmer thinks: 'well is dry' ... 'no water in well' ... 'well is no good, well is dry'
farmer throws earth on donkey in well ... farmer throws earth on donkey
donkey shakes his back ... donkey shakes his back ... earth falls ... earth falls
farmer throws earth for three hours ... donkey shakes his back for three hours ...
earth falls for three hours ...
donkey jumps out of well ... donkey jumps out of well ... donkey runs away, far away.

4. Ask the class to sit up and open their eyes. Let them see the skeleton text above.

5. Have them tell you the words they don't understand; put them on the board. Write the L1 equivalents under the English words (in small letters).

6. Ask them to write down the words they did not know. Tell them to underline them in one colour if they like the word and in another if they don't.

7. Now tell them the story in your own way in simple but full language, using mime, drawing and where necessary quick unobtrusive translations.

8. Finish the lesson by asking them, in L1, what they feel the moral of the story is. Be prepared to accept all suggestions.

40 The Story of a Mouse

Language focus:	Imagery used as a prompt for memory
Level:	Lower intermediate to advanced
Time:	30 minutes
Preparation:	None.

in class

1. Ask the students to sit comfortably and shut their eyes. Tell them to mentally focus on each hand and each finger, one after the other, and then to focus on each foot and on each toe.

2. Then tell this story, leaving long pauses, asking the students to form the best pictures they can in their minds:

   The mouse wanted to get to the sea .... She was an inland mouse ... she wanted to smell sea air ....
   She wanted to hear the waves crashing on the rocks ...
   she wanted to feel the hugeness of the sea.
   Her parents said 'No! The sea is too far away – stay at home.'
   One day the mouse said to herself: 'I'm going to the sea ...'
   On her way ... Oh, there's a cat! ...
   She darted down a hole ... she waited all night .... she was safe down the hole ...
   The mouse scuttled on ... then, Oh, there's a dog!
   She darted down a hole ....
   She came out .... she was careful to the right .... she was careful to the left ....
   She knew the world was dangerous ...
   The mouse scuttled on ....
   A screech above her ... a screech behind her ...
   A bird with claws and noisy wings ....
   The mouse darted down a hole ...
   She hid ... she waited ...
   The bird was gone ...
   The mouse scuttled on and on and on ...
   She smelled the salt in the air ...
   She heard the waves crashing on the rocks ...
   She was on a cliff above the great sea ...
   The sun was setting over the water.

3. The second time, leave out parts and elicit them from the
students. Anyone can shout out the answers. Help with gestures if
they can't think of a word.

*The mouse wanted to get to _____ .... She was an inland mouse
... she wanted to smell _____...*
She wanted to hear the waves crashing _____ ...
She wanted to feel the _____ of the sea.
Her parents said 'No! the sea is too far away, _____,'...
One day the mouse said to herself: 'I'm _____,'...
On her way, Oh, there's _____! ...
*She darted down _____ .... she waited _____ ... she was safe
down the hole ....*
The mouse scuttled on .... Oh! Then there's _____! ....
She darted down a hole ....
*She came out ... she was careful _____ .... she was careful
_____.....*
She knew the world was _____...
The mouse scuttled on ....
A screech above her .... A screech behind her ...
A _____ with claws and noisy _____ ...
The mouse darted down a hole ....
She _____ .... she waited ....
The bird _____...
The mouse scuttled on and on ...
She _____ the salt in the air ...
She heard _____ crashing on the rocks ...
She was on a cliff above _____....
The sun _____ over the water.

Acknowledgement
We learnt this story from Robert McCall, Hamburg.

41

A Nose for Bread

Language focus: Writing narrative

Level: Elementary to advanced

Time: 40–50 minutes

Preparation: None.

in class

1. Be sure the students know what *bribe* means. Invite them to relax and shut their eyes. Tell them:

   We are going to create a story together.

   'The barber sat down heavily at the breakfast table.'

   I will give you 20 seconds to imagine what the barber, Ivan Ivanovich, was like.

   'Ivan Ivanovich said, 'And how about breakfast? His wife slopped some tea into his cup. She then banged a loaf of bread down on the table.'

   I will give you 20 seconds to decide what sort of woman she is.

   'Ivan broke the loaf open and a human nose fell out on the table.'

   I will give you 20 seconds to imagine how they both reacted.

   'On his way to work Ivan Ivanovich had to cross the River Neva. He was very afraid.'

   20 seconds to see the situation in your mind's eye.

   'He was arrested and the police officer refused the bribe he offered him.'

   20 seconds to finish your story.

2. Ask the students to work individually and write the story they have imagined.

3. Each student gives his story to another, who reads it carefully. They sit with a new partner and re-tell the other student's story.

Acknowledgement
This is a version of a story by Gogol.

A Day in the Life of ...

Language focus:	Reading comprehension, narrating daily events
Level:	Lower intermediate to advanced
Time:	30 minutes
Preparation:	Make copies of the text in point 6 below. Optional: computer projection of pictures at end of this activity, or printed copy.

in class

1. Show the slides (see pictures 1–4 on p.111).

2. Then ask learners the following questions, giving them time between each one to make a few notes:
   Imagine someone who is working with a volunteer organisation and living in a small Caribbean city.
   Try to think what their day would be like. Write down some ideas about each question:
   What would they do as soon as they get up?
   What kinds of things would they see in the city?
   What kinds of relationships would they have with people?
   What would they do in their free time?

3. Tell students they are going to work with a text written by Maura Varley, a Peace Corps worker in Belize, describing a typical day in her life there (Some information about the country is given at the end of this activity.)

4. Divide students into groups of four and give one of the four paragraphs of the text to each student. Have them read their paragraph silently two or three times until they are familiar with what is written. While they are doing this, they can ask you about any vocabulary they don't know.

5. Then the person with paragraph 1 begins to tell – not read – about their part of Maura's day, putting it into their own words (*She gets up at 6 and ...*).

6. Next the person with paragraph 2, and so forth. Together they reconstruct her day.

   1. I start each day at 6 a.m. with a warm bucket bath and a cup of Guatemalan coffee when I have some available. Contrary to what you may think, good coffee is hard to get in Belize and so it is a big treat. After breakfast I ride my bike across town to either Gwen Lizarraga or Excelsior High School, the two schools where I work. The city is small, so I get there in only about 15 minutes – so a

bicycle is a very useful means of transportation in the city. I don't need a car at all.

2. Part of my day is spent counseling students about their lives—giving me something new to think about every day. I may discuss Tyrone's problems with anger and his gang involvement one minute or chat with Mikal about his latest soccer triumph the next. I've discovered that beneath their tough exteriors, many troubled young people of Belize are struggling inside, hiding their sensitivity. I am lucky to be in a position to get to see this side of them. They have a hard life, although in reality, their situations are no different from underprivileged youth in the United States.

3. Much of my day is spent discussing new ideas or developing programs with the two school counselors. We also keep each other's spirits up. One of them, Carolyn, amazes me at how she can balance a life of two small children, her full-time job, and her university studies. This is a common way of life for many young professionals in Belize because education is valued so much. Belizeans love to talk, so much of my day is spent in conversation with the counselors, teachers, and school staff. This is a very accepted part of a workday.

4. At around 4 or 5 p.m., I leave for home. If I must stay late for a parents' meeting, students escort me home on their bikes. I may spend my evenings going for a run, buying fruit from a Salvadoran street vendor who greets me in Spanish, stopping for water and Creole bread from the shop around the corner, or getting the latest gossip from my neighbour who stops me to talk. After cooking and eating my dinner, I may read, write letters, or visit with friends.

7. As a follow-up you could discuss with them:
  1. *What things in the reading coincided with what they had imagined.*
  2. *How her day is different from a typical day in their life.*

Notes
Activating imagery about a topic can prepare learners for reading it. The images in their mind can help to fill in gaps in their linguistic knowledge and to narrow down possible meanings of unknown words.

Acknowledgement
We thank Maura Varley for letting us use a version of her story.

Picture 1

Picture 2

Picture 3

Picture 4

BELIZE

Belize, called British Honduras until 1981, is a small country that lies on the Caribbean side of Central America. It has many coral reefs along the coast, and 60% of the land is tropical forests.
It has a population of about 275,000 inhabitants, some of whom are descendants of the Mayan Indians who originally lived there. English is the official language, but Spanish is spoken by many people.

Picture 5

Living my Day Again

Language focus: Past tense verbs, writing

Level: Intermediate to advanced

Time: 40–50 minutes; 10 minutes in the following class

Preparation: The day before, ask the students, as a sort of game for something they'll be doing the next class, to be particularly attentive to what they do the rest of that day and the next day before class, to try to observe what they do and what they think about.

in class

Lesson 1

1. Tell students that you are going to see how good their memory is. You are going to ask them some questions about the time since the last class, and they should try to see the different moments in their minds in order to answer the questions. Tell them you will pause after each group of questions and let them write down some notes, including any small details they remember.

Remember the moment you left class. How did you feel after class? What did you do during the two hours after you left class the last day? See yourself then and write down as many things as you can …

See yourself now as you get ready for dinner. Where did you eat dinner? Who were you with? What was pleasant or unpleasant about dinner?...

What did you do after dinner? Was it what you wanted to do? Was there anything you wanted to do that you didn't do?...

As the day ended, do you consider you were happy about the day? If not, how did you feel? Why? Did you have any thoughts about the next day?...

See yourself now when you got up today. What did you think about when you woke up? How did you feel about the day ahead of you – were you excited, worried, interested? Did you have any goals or specific plans for the day?...

Try to remember all that you did so far today. What were the three most interesting things that happened? They don't have to be big or important things.

2. From their notes, the students now invent a character and write about him or her in the third person using things from their notes but adding details, events, etc. to make a good narrative of a day in the life of their character. (It may be easier to do this after having done Activity 42, A Day in the Life of ...). Have them hand in the narrative at the end of class.

Lesson 2

1. Read several of the narratives (or all, if the class size permits) aloud, to see if the class can guess who wrote them.

Variation

For informal, voluntary homework, ask students to observe themselves closely another day and check if they are able to do so with greater attention this time.

Note

If students develop their faculties for attention, learning – including language learning – will be more efficient. Strengthening attention is a positive 'side-effect' of this activity.

44

What Kind of Parent?

Language focus: Listening leading to imagery, leading to writing

Level: Elementary to advanced

Time: 30–60 minutes

Preparation: Familiarise yourself with the actions and words below, so you can do the first part of the activity.

1. Tell the students to stand up, face you and then imitate or mirror exactly what you do, and say:

Your actions	Your words
Stand in a relaxed way –	
Look at your watch, whistle	*Oh, no!*
Shake your head slowly	*He's going to be late.*
Look upward and lift your head	*John ... John!*
Cock your head in listening mode	(loudly) *John!*
Shake your head	*Wake up, John.*
Mime plodding up stairs –	(to yourself)
(do it on the spot)	*He's going to be really late ...*
Knock on 'door'	*John, get up, you're late for school!*
Knock much harder	*John, show a leg, time to go.*
Open 'door'	*What? Where's John?*
Mime listening	*Oh, sorry, you're in the bathroom ... Silly me!*

2. Thank the students for their help. Ask them to sit down and give them a moment to relax. Ask them to breathe in and then exhale very slowly five times.

3. Ask them to answer these questions in their minds, imagining a brief story of the father's life as a child:
   How old is this father?
   What was he like as a little boy?
   What was he like at school?
   What was he like as a teenager?
   How did he treat his Dad?
   How did his Dad treat him?
   What was his Mum like?

4. Now ask the students to work individually and write a one-page portrait or story of the father as a boy.

What Kind of Parent?

5. Group them in fours to read their texts and to discuss parenting. Suggest a few questions appropriate for the age of your students.

Note
If you are a woman, a 'mother' can be used instead of the 'father'.

Acknowledgement
We learnt the idea of 'group mirroring' from Bernard Dufeu.

The End of the Story

Language focus: Writing

Level: Elementary to advanced

Time: 30 minutes

Preparation: Make copies of the beginning of a story, or use the one below.

in class

1. Hand out the beginning of a story. Ask your learners to read the text. Example:

The Ghost who came out of a Book

There was once a very small ghost who lived in a book – a book of ghost stories, of course. Sometimes people caught a glimpse of it and thought it was some sort of bookmark, but mostly people did not see it at all. When anybody opened the book to read it, the ghost slipped out from between the pages and flew around the room, looking at the people and the people's things. Then, when the ghost saw that the person reading the book was growing sleepy or was finishing the story, it slid back into the book and hid between the pages again. There was one page it especially liked, with a picture of a haunted house on it.

One evening a child was reading the ghost stories and the ghost slipped out of the book as usual. It flew around the top of the room and looked at spiders' webs in the corners of the ceiling. It tugged at the webs and the spiders came out, thinking they'd caught something. Then the very small ghost shouted 'Boo!' at them, frightening them so that they ran back into their cracks and corners to hide. While the ghost was doing this, the child's mother came in, shut the book, kissed the child and put the light out, all in a second or two. The ghost was shut out of the book and left outside, in the world of the house.

'Oh well,' said the ghost, quite pleased ...

---

2. Tell your class that they are going to find out more about the curious little ghost from the story. Ask your class to have pen and paper ready. Draw a set of six picture frames on the board. Ask them to copy these onto their paper and tell them that they are going to see how the story with the ghost will continue. Then say, in a soft and gentle voice:

45 The End of the Story

You have read part of the story of the little ghost. I wonder how the story's going to continue? What will be in the first picture? Close your eyes and find out what's going to happen. Maybe you can see the picture quite clearly, or maybe you just get a vague idea of what's going to happen. Take your time and find out about it. When you have finished with picture one, open your eyes and either draw a matchstick version of the picture or write some words into frame one.

3. Give your students time. Then continue:
   Now you are going to find out about picture 2. What's in it, can you imagine? Again, take as much time as you need. Then open your eyes again and either draw picture 2 or write some words into the second frame. Take all the time you need; and then go on in the same way with the rest of the story. Close your eyes as often as you need to finish the story. Do this at your own pace.

4. When students have finished, put them into threes. Ask them to share what they have thought of, and to come up with a joint, group version of the story and decide how they want to tell it to the rest of the class.

5. Have the students form a circle with their chairs. Each group now tells their story to the class.

| Picture 1 | Picture 2 | Picture 3 | Picture 4 | Picture 5 | Picture 6 |

These drawings were created by Concha González, a student in an ELT writing class.

Variations
1. After sharing orally in groups, the students write a joint version which is circulated round the other groups.

2. After completing their six drawings, students write down their stories individually, and then in groups of three read each other's versions.

Acknowledgement
Margaret Mahy, 'The Ghost who Came out of a Book', in *Never Meddle with Magic and Other Stories* chosen by Barbara Ireson, Puffin Books, 1988.

Writing from the Sound of Music

Language focus: Writing

Level: Lower intermediate to advanced

Time: 40-50 minutes

Preparation: Select several short bits of music or use the selection on the CD. Bring in a CD player.

Track 7

in class

1. Tell students that you are going to help them to write a great story, and that you are going to do this by playing music and asking a few questions

2. Play the first bit of music, and as students listen ask the following questions:

   Try to see a movie in your mind. Where is this?
   Who do you see? What do the people look like? Is there anything special about them? What are they doing?
   Are they outside or inside? What is the place like?
   What can you hear?
   Can you smell anything there?
   What is the weather like? Warm or cold?

3. When the music stops, put the CD on pause and have students write down a few things about the movie they had in their mind as they listened to the music and thought about the questions.

4. Play the next parts, asking each time: *What is happening now?* Add any other questions you think might help your students create their story (*Who appears? How do they react? Where do they go now? Why are they going there? How does this end? ...*) Pause after each piece of music for them to write down some details of what they are imagining.

5. Have students go back over their notes and then write their story. When they finish, ask them to work in group of threes and pass their stories to each other to read. Students may be interested in seeing how, starting from the same stimuli, they end up with often quite different stories.

Note
Music has a great facility for producing images and connecting with our emotions. For this reason, it is very useful for the idea-generation phase of writing activities.

Acknowledgement
We first saw this done by Carmen Fonseca.

47 Guided Writing

Language focus: Speaking and writing

Level: Lower intermediate to advanced

Time: 40-50 minutes

Preparation: None.

in class

1. Put students in pairs, or ask them to move round the room and pair off when you say stop. When the pairs sit down, they face each other.

2. Explain to the students that person A in the pair is to bring to mind an older person they know well – an aunt, a grandparent etc. Ask them to think how this person would be dressed, how their voice would sound and how they would sit.

3. Tell the As to sit like the person they have brought to mind and to enter the role of this person. Student B interviews them for 5 minutes about their life.

4. Then they change and student B role-plays an elderly person they know.

5. Now explain that each person in the pair is to write a page in role as their partner's older person. They write in the first person. They are to try and write in the same kind of voice that their partner used to role-play the old person. Allow 10-15 minutes for the writing.

6. The partners read their texts to each other and comment on whether the writer has captured the feeling of the older person role-played.

Variation
This can also be done having students think of other people they know (a good friend, for example) or someone they don't know (a well-known person) but where they can imagine what their life is like, and to answer in role.

Writing from Illustrations

Language focus: Writing

Level: Lower intermediate to advanced

Time: 40–50 minutes in one class and 15–30 minutes in another

Preparation: Bring in a computer projector or make a printed copy of the pictures to show.

in class

Lesson 1

1. Paintings or photos can be a great stimulus for ELT writing. Outside the classroom, normally a story would be written first and then illustrations added. Here we are going to do the opposite: give students some illustrations and then let them create a story from their imagination. Show the illustrations, and ask these or other questions you would like to use. Let them make notes after each one. You may find it useful to show the pictures a second time.

Picture 1

We are going to see some pictures. Try to create a movie in your mind about what is happening: Imagine the building this is in. Who lives here? Have the people just arrived home or just left? What does the street outside look like? What has just happened here?

Picture 2

Who are these people? Why are they here? What are they talking about? What do they do normally?

Picture 3

Where is this telephone? Who is going to use it to call someone? Who are they going to call? What are they going to say?

Picture 4

What has happened before this scene? Where does this corridor lead to?

Picture 5

Who uses this garage? Is someone going into the garage? Coming out of it?

Picture 6

Who does this car belong to? Where is it going? Why?

Picture 7

Where is this scene? What happens here?

2. Have students write stories based on their notes, using most if not all the scenes. Collect and correct them.

Lesson 2

1. At the beginning of class you may want to have students rewrite their stories, incorporating the corrections. Then have them work in groups of three. They each read the other two stories, and discuss what they have in common and what is different.

2. Then have each group tell the whole class one thing they found in common and one difference.

SECTION 4
IMAGES OF TIME AND SPACE

My Favourite Places

Language focus:	Describing environments
Level:	Elementary to advanced
Time:	20-30 minutes
Preparation:	None.

in class

1. Ask the students to sit comfortably and close their eyes if they wish; tell them they are going to think of three places:

   First of all, think of your favourite place in your house or flat.

   Notice the light in this favourite place, and the colours.

   Notice what you can hear in this place.

   How does it feel to be here?

   Secondly, maybe there is street, a corner, a square, a place by the water that you like in your town or your village.

   Is your picture of this place calm or busy ... or something else?

   The smells in this place ... the temperature?

   This place in summer ... in spring ... in winter?

   Finally, can you remember a recent holiday you liked?

   Is there a place you went to on this holiday that felt really good?

   What does it look like? How big is the picture you have created in your head?

   How near is the picture to you?

   Can you observe sounds? ... Noises? ... Voices close by? ... Voices far away? ... Animal noises? ... Planes overhead?

   How would this place be at a different time of year from when you went?

   What would you change in this place to make it better?

2. Bring the students back from their thoughts and randomly pair them.

3. Tell the pairs they have 90 seconds each to describe their first place, in their home. Time them, and shout out *90 seconds!* when it is time for them to swap. Stop them at the end of the 3 minutes. Then tell them to move around the room before re-pairing with a new person.

4. Again give them 3 minutes for description of the second place.

5. Repeat for the third place.

Note
Limiting the time for an oral activity can be a powerful way of helping students concentrate, and say more and say it better.

Acknowledgement
The idea of working on favourite places comes from Christine Frank et. al., *Grammar in Action Again*, Prentice Hall, 1987.

Letting the Images Flow

Language focus: Speaking

Level: Lower intermediate to advanced

Time: 15 minutes

Preparation: Optional: bring in a CD player.

in class

1. Have the students sitting in pairs facing each other and if possible not too close to other pairs. If numbers are uneven, be prepared to participate yourself. It is often useful if you demonstrate first with a volunteer, so students will understand when you give them the instructions below.

2. Ask them to sit comfortably and, in a gentle voice, say:

   In a moment you are going to turn on your mental visual screen. Then you will wait until one of you sees or senses a place. It may be real or imagined, a place where you live, a place you have travelled to, a place you have seen in a film, or a place you totally invent. You'll begin describing it to your partner, saying two or three sentences, and then stopping. Your partner will take over and continue describing what you began, adding two or three sentences, and then stopping. Go back and forth a few times, following the stream of images you are producing. It is easier if you close your eyes. Now, let's go. Turn on your mental screens and begin.

3. Give them 4–5 minutes. Then quietly tell them they can take one more minute to finish.

4. Have each pair describe their imagined place to another pair. Afterwards, with the whole class, talk about how easy or difficult it was and how they felt as they did it.

Variation
1. Weather and situation permitting, this activity can be done outside for even better results.

2. For a very different effect it can be done as an online project, pairing students in a different class/city/country. Using a chat format, they take turns to develop the image stream. They can print the final product or write it out by hand and bring it in to class to be made up into a poster or a photocopied class publication. (Suggested by Javier Ávila.)

Note

We learnt a version of this activity from Tim Murphey (1998a:10). He explains that the theory behind an image streaming activity is that it 'connects different parts of our brains through words and visualisation, stimulating new connections and new learning'. At the same time it adds a great amount of personal meaning to the task at hand. Jane did this with a group of MA students in the Canary Islands and with one of the pairs the first student began describing a walk through Seville, where he had studied some years before. It turned out that his partner had also studied there and so he added things he remembered to the image stream. Afterwards they commented how much they had enjoyed being able to 'return' there in this activity.

51 Remember Then

Language focus: Past tenses, writing, speaking

Level: Lower intermediate to advanced

Time: 30–40 minutes

Preparation: Be prepared to tell your class about some moments from your childhood. Photo on computer for projection, or have a large photo of a school in the past. Alternatively, begin with step 3.

in class

1. Show the photo on a computer projector or show your photo of a school in the past.

2. If using this photo, tell students that this was a school in Kansas in 1925. Ask them to write down how it is different from the school they knew as a child, and what they imagine these children's lives were like. Working in pairs, they share ideas with their partner.

3. Tell the class something you remember about your childhood. Then individually, learners make a list of 8 categories of things they can remember about their childhood. For example, student A might list *my favourite toy, what I liked for breakfast, a friend, my favourite teacher* …

4. Sitting with their partner, using their own list of things, the As ask the Bs to tell them what the Bs remember about each of the categories the As have written on their lists. The As would do this in the following way:

Remember your childhood and tell me about your favourite toy ...
Remember your childhood and tell me about what you liked for breakfast ...
Remember your childhood and tell me about a friend ...

5. Then the Bs ask the As to talk about the things on the Bs' own lists. After they have both remembered, they can discuss the experience briefly.

Acknowledgement

Jean Houston (1982: 87–8) developed an exercise similar to this because she noticed how people with good memories tended to recall images and events from their childhood and she affirms that when we activate 'childhood memories we apparently prime the memory banks generally, so that regular practice brings with it a substantial improvement in all aspects of memory and recall'.

52 Starting from Spaces

Language focus:	Descriptive writing
Level:	Lower intermediate to advanced
Time:	40 minutes
Preparation:	None.

in class

1. Tell the class:

   Close your eyes if you wish and notice your breathing. Listen to all you can hear inside your body or outside the room. I'm going to ask you now to imagine some different spaces …

   Leave about 10 seconds between each of the phrases

   Coming out of a forest

   Walking beside a small river

   Sitting on a hilltop

   Listening to the wind blowing in off the sea

   Crossing a square in a city

   Looking out from a 10th-floor city flat

   Searching for something in a dark place

   In an armchair at home

   In bed in a strange place.

2. Ask each student to work on their own and choose three of the above spaces, and write a paragraph about each.

3. Put them into groups of four and they read their texts to the group.

53 Going up in a Balloon

Language focus: Lexical set of geographical features; action verbs, revision of present progressive

Level: Lower intermediate to intermediate

Time: 15-20 minutes

Preparation: Optional: bring in a CD player.

in class

1. Pre-teach a lexical set for geographical features, such as *city, town, village, street, motorway, market square, lane, hill, mountain, cliff, river, lake, pond, sea, coast, beach, wood, forest, field, park* etc.

2. Ask your students if in their dreams or daydreams they ever have the sensation of flying. Ask them to sit comfortably, and either play CD track no. 8 or say, in a quiet voice:

    I'd like you to imagine that you can see a very colourful hot-air balloon now. It's a beautiful day. We are on a beach somewhere. We walk towards the balloon. You are now invited to get into the basket, and we are going to go up in the balloon.

    We are gently going up ... it's a wonderful sensation ... there is a light breeze ... When you look down you can see a nice little wood ... next to it there are some cornfields ... and there is a meadow close to it ... there are some people ... they are playing a ball game ... at some distance from the group there is a man behind an ice-cream kiosk ... you can see some children queuing up for the ice cream ...

    Now as you look out towards the other side of the balloon you can see the sea ... there are a few sailing boats and people on their surfboards ... they are enjoying the breeze ... surfing up and down the coast ...

3. Ask your students to come back to the here and now of the classroom. Tell them that you want them to work in pairs and guide each other in their imagination, going up in a balloon, or flying a glider or a hang glider. Tell them they can guide their partner through a place they know or an invented one.

4. If necessary, write language prompts on the board. Example:

You're	*flying over a city.*
We're	*going in our balloon over a …*
I'm	*getting closer to a …*

I can see some cars. They're driving towards …
A sports car's overtaking …

Below me/us/you there's a group of young people.
They're (riding their bikes).

5. Give students some time to take turns guiding each other in their imagination. Later, they can go back to the visualisation in their imagination and write a text as if they were still flying. (E.g. *Now I'm in a little glider. I'm flying my plane over a beautiful landscape. I can see some people. They're …*)

The Lake in the Wood

Language focus: Writing in a strict poetic form (*haiku*)

Level: Lower intermediate to advanced

Time: 40–50 minutes

Preparation: Make a copy of this haiku poem for each of your students:

> *An old silent pond ...*
> *A frog jumps into the pond,*
> *splash! Silence again.*

Optional: bring in a CD player

in class

1. Hand out the poem to your students. After they have read it, explain that the poem is a haiku, and that traditional Japanese haiku poems were composed in three lines with 5-7-5 syllables. The poems generally describe very briefly a place, real or imagined, often with reference to nature or one of the seasons. When people started writing English haiku in the 1950s, they adopted this 5-7-5 form. This style is often called *Traditional English haiku*. Over the years, poets have come to write haiku in fewer syllables in English, most often in three segments that follow a short-long-short pattern without such a rigid structure. Some people call this style 'free-form' haiku. The poem your students have read is the translation of a haiku by Matsuo Basho (1644–1694).

2. Ask your students to read the haiku again. Ask them to sit in a relaxed way and close their eyes. They should imagine the situation the haiku describes. Either play CD track no. 9 or, in a calm and quiet voice, say:

Whatever you are thinking right now ... allow yourself to focus your attention on yourself ... and when you have some distracting thoughts ... acknowledge them ... and gently turn your attention back to yourself ... And feel your contact with the chair you are sitting on ... and feel the contact of your feet with the floor and the ground below you ... And you might still have some thoughts and memories that distract you ... acknowledge them and let them go ... like a cloud that appears in the sky ... and vanishes again ... Allow yourself to be centred and focussed.

I'd like to invite you to come for a short walk with me ... to a beautiful place in a wood ... feel the soft ground beneath your feet as you are walking along ... smell the fresh scent of the leaves ... listen to the sound of silence ... only occasionally interrupted by the beautiful song of a bird ... And as you are walking along, you can see that there is a clearing in front of you ... and you can see the light of the sun ahead ... and as you are walking closer to the clearing ... you can see a beautiful lake ... and the reflection of the sunlight on the surface of the water ...

You are standing right in front of the lake now ... it's a beautiful place ... so calm ... the surface of the water is so still ... Look around yourself ... until you can see some pebbles on the ground ... select a small and beautiful pebble ... pick it up ... look at it ... hold it towards the sun ... then throw it out towards the middle of the lake ... you can hear the pebble plop into the water ... it's sinking deeper and deeper ... you can see the ripples ... spreading out in all directions ... the pebble is going deeper and deeper ... the waves are spreading out wider and wider ... deeper and deeper ... wider and wider ...

3. Ask your students to stay calm within themselves for some time. Then encourage them to write their own haiku based on the experience of their mental imagery.

If you wish, play music as they write. Tell students that they should make their haiku a 'picture with words'. They should not put their names on the papers.

4. If you want to give another example of a haiku, create one yourself, or use the following written by a student in one of Herbert's classes:

> *Held close to my eye,*
> *a little round pebble*
> *covers up the sun.*

5. Later, ask students to stick all their haikus on a wall of the classroom. Students walk round and read the poems. Then they comment on which poem they believe was written by who, and why.

Shapes in Spaces

Language focus:	Vocabulary revision
Level:	Elementary to intermediate
Time:	10–15 minutes
Preparation:	To revise words for shapes and prepositions of place, one copy of the shapes worksheet (at the end of this activity) for each student. Alternatively, select a lexical set you want to revise with your students, and draw a worksheet based on principles similar to the shapes one. For the variation, a copy of the map for each student.

in class

1. Hand out a copy of the worksheet (at the end of this activity) to each student. Explain that you will give them a few minutes for them to try to remember in their mind's eye the drawings in each space on the worksheet as precisely as possible. Model how they should look at the first drawing, close their eyes and try to remember it with their eyes closed, open their eyes again to check whether their internal picture was correct, close their eyes again and open them again. They should do this for each of the eight pictures, revising also the ones they've already stored in their mind.

2. Explain that now they are to listen with their eyes closed, and you will describe one of the pictures. They should imagine it with their eyes closed, then open their eyes and write down the number you have given for the picture in the box they think was described.

3. Ask them to close their eyes. In a quiet voice, say:

    In picture 1 there is a grey rectangle. On top of it there is a grey circle. On top of the grey circle there is a black triangle.

    Once more: in picture 1 there's a grey rectangle. On top of it there's a grey circle. On top of the grey circle there's a black triangle. Now open your eyes. Look for the right picture and write 1 on it. Close your eyes again.

    In picture 2 there's a white circle within a black octagon. On top of the octagon there's a black triangle.

    Once more: in picture 2 there's a white circle within a black octagon. On top of the octagon there's a black triangle. Now open your eyes. Look for the right picture and write 2 on it. Close your eyes again.

    In picture 3 there's a black triangle in between a white square and a grey circle.

Once more: in picture 3 there's a black triangle in between a white square and a grey circle. Now open your eyes. Look for the right picture and write 3 on it. Close your eyes again.

In picture 4 there's a grey rectangle. On top of the grey rectangle there's a grey circle. On top of the grey circle there's a black triangle, and it's upside down.

Once more: in picture 4 there's a grey rectangle. On top of the grey rectangle there's a grey circle. On top of the grey circle there's a black triangle, and it's upside down. Now open your eyes. Look for the right picture and write 4 on it. Close your eyes again.

In picture 5 there's a black circle within a grey octagon. On top of the grey octagon there's a grey triangle.

Once more: in picture 5 there's a black circle within a grey octagon. On top of the grey octagon there's a grey triangle. Now open your eyes. Look for the right picture and write 5 on it. Close your eyes again.

In picture 6 there's a white ellipsis on top of a grey triangle. On the left-hand side of the white ellipsis there's a grey pentagon.

Once more: in picture 6 there's a white ellipsis on top of a grey triangle. On the left-hand side of the white ellipsis there's a grey pentagon. Now open your eyes. Look for the right picture and write 6 on it. Close your eyes again.

In picture 7 there's a grey triangle on top of a white ellipsis. On the right-hand side of the white ellipsis there's a grey pentagon.

Once more: In picture 7 there's a grey triangle on top of a white ellipsis. On the right-hand side of the white ellipsis there's a grey pentagon. Now open your eyes. Look for the right picture and write 7 on it. Close your eyes again.

In picture 8 there's a grey triangle in between a black square and a grey circle.

Once more: in picture 8 there's a grey triangle in between a black square and a grey circle. Now open your eyes. Look for the right picture and write 8 on it.

4. Tell them the solutions. Then ask students to work in pairs. Student A closes their eyes, Student B describes one of the pictures to A. A listens with their eyes closed, then opens their eyes and says, e.g. *It's picture number 3.*

Worksheet

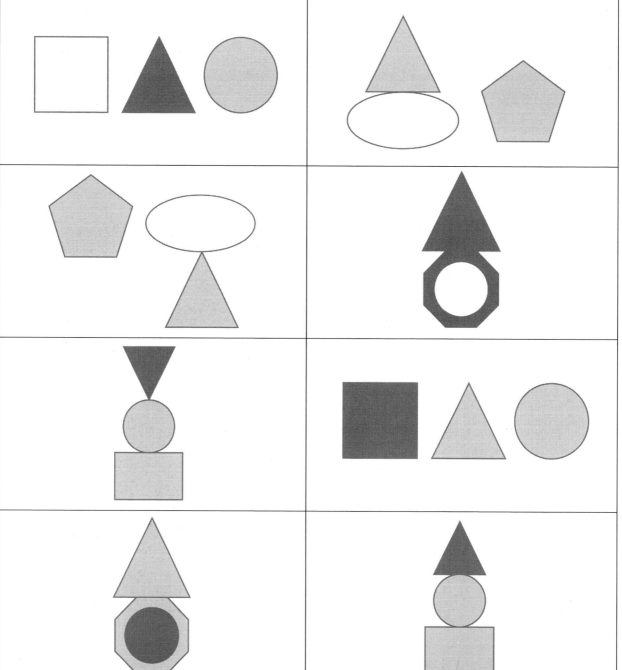

Variation

Give each student a copy of a map. The map needs a START position clearly indicated. Give your students time to look at the map and remember it visually. Ask them to close their eyes. Give them directions to your 'home', e.g. *You are at START ('You are here') now. Walk straight ahead, take the first right, go straight again, turn left after the bookshop. I live opposite the cinema, above the cafe.*

Ask students to open their eyes and describe the way to where you live. Later, the activity can be done in pairs, with each one choosing a place to be where they live and giving instructions as in the example above.

Where Animals Live

Language focus: Description of inner pictures

Level: Lower intermediate to advanced

Time: 5 minutes in one class (for lower levels) and 20-30 minutes in the next

Preparation: None.
For the variation, photocopies of the chart.

in class

Lesson 1 (for lower levels)

1. Review the names of all the animals you decide to use in the guided visualisation lesson that follows. To fix any words the students don't know well, have them classify the words into three groups: animals that live on land, animals that live at least partly in the water and animals that fly.

Lesson 2

1. Tell the students you are going to ask them to relax, and shut their eyes if they wish. Tell them you will give them the name of an animal followed by a 10-second pause for them to picture the place or places where they might see this animal, the place it lives in, and all the environment it moves around in.

2. Say these animals, pausing for 10 seconds between each:
   camel
   goldfish
   rattlesnake
   eagle
   mosquito
   duck
   kangaroo
   bee
   cow
   shark
   frog
   butterfly

3. Ask students to decide which animal name gave them the most vivid idea of a place or environment, and ask them to get into pairs and describe what they saw, heard and felt as clearly as they can to their partner. You can consider the option of having them link up with another person who chose the same animal.

56 Where Animals Live

Variation
Give each student a copy of the chart and have them fill in the first column with their own answers and then interview their partner.

	Me	My partner
Which animal brought you the brightest, most colourful picture?		
Did you see yourself with any animal? Which one?		
Which animal had you hearing the most sounds?		
Which animal brought you the most smells?		
Which animal made you most aware of heat?		
Which animal made you most aware of cold?		
Which animal had you feeling the weather most?		
Which animal would you most like to see?		

Night-Time Experiences

Language focus: Narrating a personal experience

Level: Lower intermediate to advanced

Time: 30 minutes

Preparation: Prepare to tell the group about a night-time experience of your own.

1. Ask your class to sit comfortably, shut their eyes and try to imagine what you're going to say. Pause between each phrase:

   The sun is going down ... the night is coming ...
   dew on the grass ... water on the grass ...
   street lamps come on ... yellowy light ...
   car headlights ...
   full moon ... moving clouds ...
   moonlight coming and going ...
   night wind ...
   cool ... cold ...
   bats in the air ...
   People going home ... people tired ... off to bed ...
   House lights going out ...
   Distant city noises ... quiet nearby ...
   Night ... night ... night.

2. Wait a few seconds and tell them a night-time experience of yours.

3. Now group them in fours to tell each other a night-time experience where they were afraid. Encourage the listeners to ask the teller questions about it.

58

Living the Seasons

Language focus: Vocabulary related to weather and climate

Level: Elementary to advanced

Time: 35–40 minutes

Preparation: Come to class ready to tell students about a day when the weather was perfect for you. Also, choose the four most weather-interesting months where your students live.

in class

1. With a student 'secretary' at the board, brainstorm words around *Climate*. Allow people to shout out L1 words as well as English ones. They may have to come up and write these down themselves, if the group is multi-mother-tongued.

2. With your help and the help of dictionaries, the words on the board are all turned into English.

3. Help the students to relax, with their eyes shut if they wish, and tell them about a day on which the weather was perfect for you. Then explain that you are going to ask them to experience the weather they expect for each month you mention:

   June; please think about the weather in June. Think of a typical day – the length of the day ... the kind of light ... is it wet or dry? How hot is it early and late? What clothes do you wear for this weather? What are the sounds of the weather in June? How do you feel in June?

   10–15 second pause

4. Repeat this for three other months. After your suggestion for each month, leave a 10–15 second pause.

5. Ask various students in the class to pick one of the months and tell the whole group about their experience of it. They may be short of vocabulary ... help them when necessary. Add to the words on the board any new words that come up.

6. Ask the students to categorise the words on the board in terms of the four months of the year you have used. They work on this individually. Then ask them to compare their categorisations in groups of four.

There was a Bright, Bright Universe

Language focus: Imaginative writing

Level: Elementary to intermediate

Time: 30–40 minutes

Preparation: Optional: bring in a CD player.

in class

1. Ask the students to tense their arm muscles and relax them four times, then do the same with shoulder muscles and leg muscles.

2. Ask them to sit comfortably and relax. Either play CD track no. 11 or read them this text in a bright, gentle voice, pausing after each phrase for a few seconds:

   There was a bright, bright universe ...
   There was a bright, bright galaxy ...
   There was a bright, bright planet ...
   There was a bright, bright continent ...
   There was a bright, bright country ...
   There was a bright, bright county ...
   There was a bright, bright valley ...
   There was a bright, bright town ...
   There was a bright, bright suburb ...
   There was a bright, bright street ...
   There was a bright, bright house ...
   There was a bright, bright kitchen ...

3. Gently bring the students back from the visualisation, and ask them to work on their own and write a half-page text, the content of which is entirely up to them.

4. Ask the students to get up, pick up their texts, move round the room and read to each other what they have written.

Acknowledgement
We learnt this story in a drama group at the Waldorf English Week in Altenberg, Germany, November 2006.

60 The Time Machine

Language focus: Speaking and writing

Level: Intermediate to advanced

Time: 20 minutes

Preparation: Optional: bring in a CD player.

in class

1. Either play CD track no. 12, or tell your students:

Sit quietly and to try to imagine how life was at different moments in history, maybe the days of the cave people ... the ancient Chinese cultures ... Roman times ... the medieval world ... the Renaissance ... the colonisation of the new world ... the Industrial Revolution ... the Far West ... the beginning of the 20th century ... the times of your grandparents .... Now try to imagine what life will be like in the distant future ... maybe on the moon or another planet.

Choose a moment that particularly interests you; it can be in the past or the future. Keep this moment in mind as you see yourself walking out of this room and going in the direction of your home. On the way you notice something you have never seen before. It is a large, very strange machine with a door. You open the door and step in. There are many buttons inside, with periods of time written on them. You realise this is a time machine and you can travel to any moment you want. There is a sign that says that after a short visit you will return to the present. You decide to go to the moment in time that you were interested in. You push the right button and off you go. In a second you are there. The door opens and you walk out. Take 3 minutes, which is all the time you need, to visit this moment and find out what it is like to live then.

3-minute pause

Now you return to the time machine, get in, close the door and push the button that says 'The Present', and you return to this room.

2. Have students get up and walk around, telling each other about the time they visited. If any chose the same time, they can compare what they saw.

3. If you wish, as a written follow-up they can describe what they saw and how they liked visiting that time. What things about today's world would they miss there? What would they like to bring to the present from the time they visited?

Variation

This activity can be used for working with CLIL (content and language integrated learning). If you teach in a secondary school, try asking your colleagues teaching history, art, literature, or science about what your students have been working on recently. Adapt the time-machine visit to the content of one or more of their other subjects. After the visit, you can ask your students to find more information about the time and place visited and then write an essay or a story about it incorporating knowledge from the content area.

61 From Sound to Picture: a Building Site

Language focus:	Making descriptions
Level:	Intermediate to advanced
Time:	20–30 minutes
Preparation:	None.

in class

1. Ask the students to shut their eyes and to sit comfortably.

   Imagine you have a brand new room in a brand new house …
   You are lying on a new bed with your head on a soft pillow …
   You can hear a small bird singing outside the freshly painted window …
   A faint smell of new paint everywhere …
   Think back to one year ago when there were no houses here … just a green field …
   Quiet voices … men and women … moving papers … the sounds of building plans unfolding …
   Notice your pictures.

   Pause

   The roar of machines digging … the sound of earth falling into lorries …
   Notice your pictures.

   Pause

   The shouts of workers … the noise of shovels.
   The roar of engines … the scream of saws … the banging of hammers.

   Pause

   Quiet … distant sounds … birdsong … a bus a mile away.

2. Bring the students back to the classroom. Put these questions on the board, and ask students to write a short answer to each:

   1 Where do you imagine this building site is – in your own country or somewhere else?
   2 In a valley … on a hillside … somewhere flat?
   3 What season is it? How do you know?
   4 And how about the weather? Wet or dry … cold or hot … foggy or clear?

5 *What kind of building site is it? Flats ... houses ... skyscrapers ... a factory?*

6 *What are the people on the site like? Male or female ... well-dressed or in rags ... happy-looking or depressed?*

7 *How does the foreman treat the workmen? How do the architects treat the foreman and the workers?*

8 *What sounds were easiest for you to hear?*

3. Tell students to write two more questions related to the topic. Working in pairs, students compare their answers to the first seven questions, and then ask each other their own two questions.

SECTION 5
SPINNING INWARD

62 Best Friends

Language focus: Language of reasoning

Level: Lower intermediate to advanced

Time: 30–50 minutes

Preparation: Optional: bring in a CD player.

in class

1. Ask students to take pen and paper, and draw a quick mind map where they list five things that make a good friend. You may want to give them an example:

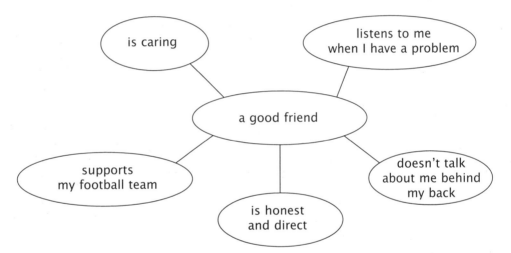

2. Give your students a few minutes to finish their mind map. Then ask them to choose from the five aspects they have recorded the one that they consider most important in a friend. Ask each student to complete the following sentence (you may want to explain the common use of 'they' as a singular neutral-gender pronoun):
   The most important thing about a friend is that they ...

3. Discuss with your class the saying *nobody's perfect*. Get them to think of something that their best friend sometimes does, or a way in which he/she sometimes behaves, which they don't like. Ask students to complete the sentence:
   I don't like it when my friend ...

4. Ask the students if it was easy or difficult for them to think of something that they didn't like about their friends.

5. Then either play CD track no. 13 or guide them in a visualisation about their best friend:

SECTION 5: SPINNING INWARD

As you are sitting there ... listening to my voice ... I would like to invite you to think of your best friend ... and imagine what your friend looks like ... the way your best friend talks ... and laughs ... the way your best friend walks and stands and sits ... and I would like you to imagine that for a few minutes ... you become your best friend ... and you see the world through the eyes of your best friend ...

And as you are now slowly becoming your best friend ... What does the world look like for you? ... What things do you like? .... What foods do you like eating? .... What's your favourite music? ... And what sport do you like playing? ... Just take your time ...

And now imagine that you really are your best friend ... and with the eyes of your best friend ... you can see yourself ... you can see the person who is you ... What is it that you like about this person who is you? And is there anything that you don't like about this person, maybe? Is there anything that this person sometimes does that you don't like, or are there ways this person who is yourself behaves that you don't like? ... Take your time to find out ...

6. Bring students back to the classroom, and ask them to complete the following sentence (to be shared then in small groups): *With my friends I sometimes ...*

7. Then ask them to think of what they need to try to do in order to become a better friend, and to complete the following sentence: *To be a better friend, I could ...*

8. Ask the students to share their findings in their groups, checking to see if they have things in common. Call on each group, to compare results between the groups.

Variation
In the last part of class or the next day try the following:

Have students work in pairs and prepare a role play of a 'difficult situation' between two friends, drawing perhaps on the previous discussions. After practising a little, each pair presents their role-play to the class. At the end of each role-play, the students get a few minutes to discuss the presentation with their partner and suggest 'solutions'. If you wish, the pair who presented the difficult situation can then role-play one of the solutions spontaneously for the class.

Acknowledgment
The activity draws heavily on suggestions in the article 'Perfect Partners', by Patrick Costello, Jan Jones and Paula Walsh, in *Teaching Thinking*, Issue 2, Autumn 2000.

63 Me in the Future

Language focus:	Descriptive writing
Level:	Intermediate to advanced
Time:	30–40 minutes
Preparation:	None.

in class

1. Say to your students:

Relax, and close your eyes if you wish. In this exercise you are going to be seeing yourself in a future time of your choice. You will decide how far forward in the future you want to see yourself. You will choose the time.

I want you to visualise a door. Notice its shape and colours.

Prepare to open the door.

Open the door and become aware of a person standing with their back to you –

This is you in the future, at the time in the future you have chosen.

Notice any sounds you can hear in this future place.

Does it feel calm or windy?

What is your nose telling you in this future place?

The person with their back to you, the future you, turns to their right.

Notice their profile, from head to toe.

What's different from you now?

The future you turns to face the now you.

What's different?

The future you says something ...

Can you answer?

Leave where you are, and step into the future you.

Become this new you –

Notice how you feel in this changed body, in this new version of you.

Notice how are you are standing, how your clothes feel, how your way of seeing may be different.

Come back into your now self –

Say goodbye to the future self –

When you are ready, come back into the room.

2. Leave the students the time to be alone with themselves for a moment.

3. Randomly pair them, then ask the students **not** to sit with their new partners.

4. Ask each person to spend 10–15 minutes writing a letter to his/her partner about the experience they had during the guided-imagery activity. The partners come together in pairs, exchange letters and then comment orally as they wish.

Variation
End the class with students silently writing feedback sentences on the board.

64

What's Happiness?

Language focus: Appreciating the language in a poem, responding to it in a self-reflexive way

Level: Intermediate to advanced

Time: 40–50 minutes

Preparation: A copy of the poem *The Happiness of Fish*, below, for each student. Also make for each student a copy of the box with questions below (unless you prefer to write them on the board).
Optional: bring in a CD player.

1. Hand out a copy of the poem, and tell your students to read it.

The Happiness of Fish
Chuang Tzu and Hue Tzu
were walking on the bridge
over the Hao river.
Chuang said:
'See how the small fish
leap and dart about.
That is the happiness of fish.'
Hue replied:
'Since you are not a fish
how can you know
the happiness of fish?'
Chuang said:
'Since you are not I
how can you know
that I do not know
the happiness of fish?'
Hue replied:
'If I, not being you,
cannot know what you know,
it follows that you,
not being a fish,
cannot know the happiness of fish.'
Chuang said:
'Wait! Let us go back
to your original question.
You asked me how I know
the happiness of fish.
The words of your question
show you knew that I know
the happiness of fish.
I know their happiness
from my own happiness
as I walk over the bridge
and see them leap and play.'
Chuang Tzu, China
(translated by Robert Fisher)

2. Then ask them questions to make sure they understand the poem and to start thinking about its meaning, for example:

Who do you think Chuang Tzu and Hue Tzu were?

Why did Chuang think the fish were happy?

What did Hue think?

What did Chuang say to try to persuade Hue that he could not know what Chuang knew?

Do you think Chuang's argument was a good one? Why (not)?

What's Happiness?

At the end of the poem, how does Chuang explain how he knows the happiness of fish?

Do you think Chuang was right in saying he knew that the fish were happy? Why?

3. Ask your students to sit comfortably, and either play CD track no. 14 or, in a quiet, calm voice, say:

As you are sitting there with your eyes open or closed ... I'd like to invite you to go back in time ... and think of a situation where you were very happy ... or, if you prefer, go to an imaginary place where you can be perfectly happy ... Wherever you have decided to go ... whether it's a place you've been to before ... or whether it's a place that you're creating now in your imagination ... allow yourself to feel that you're fully there, in that place of perfect happiness.

Take your time to become aware what that place looks like ... whether the place is somewhere out of doors or in a closed room ... and if you are alone or if there are other people with you ... and if there are other people with you, who they are ... and what they are doing ... And I wonder what kind of sounds you can hear in your place of perfect happiness ... whether there is any music ... or there are people's voices ... or the sounds of nature ...

And now ... I'd like to ask you to feel this feeling of happiness ... and notice how you can feel it ... and become aware, as well, if you are with other people or with another person, whether there is happiness in those other people who are with you ... And now I'd like you to imagine that from that place of happiness you are looking back over your life ... like in a film ... a film of happiness ... and you can see all the situations in which you were happy ... Just notice them, as they come and go in your memory ... notice where you were, and how you were feeling happy, and who you were with, and what you heard and did and saw ... And notice whether these situations have anything in common ... or maybe they are all completely different ... just notice those situations ... before you come back to this classroom and open your eyes again.

4. Hand out the questions below, unless you've written them on the board, and ask students to silently think about them for a few minutes, and jot down any thoughts they have on a piece of paper.

64 What's Happiness?

> - What does it mean to be happy? Can you give examples of being happy?
> - When you say you are happy, how do you know you are happy?
> - Do you know when other people are happy? Do you know if animals are happy?
> - Is feeling you are happy the same as knowing you are happy?
> - If you are not happy, are you unhappy? Are there different kinds of happiness?
> - Do you always know how you are feeling?
> - Could you be happy all the time? Why (not)?
> - Can other people make you happy or can you only make yourself happy? Explain.

5. Then ask them to discuss their answers, either as a whole class or in groups which later report their findings to the class.

Variation

As an alternative or additional idea to begin the activity, ask your students some time before the lesson to bring photographs to class of themselves in situations in which they were happy.

Ask them to put their photos on the floor of the classroom and sit around them. Pick up one photograph, ask whose it is and hand it round the circle.

Get your students each to imagine a brief background story to that photograph. If they find this difficult, give an example, for instance: *Carlos, I think this photograph shows you a few years ago, with some friends. I think when the photo was taken you were about 12. You seem very happy and relaxed – maybe you were going to have a picnic and you were looking forward to it.*

After several interpretations of the picture have been heard, ask the student whose picture it is to explain what the situation was really like.

Acknowledgment

The poem and the questions used in the activity are from *Poems for Thinking*, by Robert Fisher, Nash Pollock Publishing,1997, pp. 46 and 47. Robert Fisher recommends using poems as a basis for developing children's and young students' thinking skills, and he stresses the need for giving students enough 'thinking time' before they are supposed to articulate their thoughts.

Mother Tongue as a Resource State

Language focus: Listening and writing

Level: Lower intermediate to advanced

Time: 25–35 minutes, and, two weeks later, 5–10 minutes

Preparation: Bring in a large envelope.

Lesson 1

1. Ask the students to sit comfortably and to close their eyes. Then say:

Imagine the sounds of your mother tongue ... think of some of the strong sounds ...
Hear some of the soft sounds ...
Hear rising sounds ... hear falling sounds ...
Hear some words from your language spoken by someone in your family who you love ...
Hear the same words again, louder and spoken from nearer to you ...
Get yourself a picture of some words in your language, words written by someone you like ...
Bring to mind a bit of text in your own language that you know by heart ...
Listen to it in your mind's ear ...
Now bring to mind a time when you spoke to someone in your own language and you spoke very well. What you said was rich ... what you said was fluent ... what you said was very clear ...

Pause

The other person showed that they liked what you said ... what you said had the effect you wanted.
Notice your feeling when you speak well ...
Notice how your voice sounds when you speak well.
Notice the pictures in your head when you speak well ...
Imagine a future time: you are speaking to someone in English and you are speaking ... well ...

Pause

... and you have positive pictures in your mind, and your voice sounds really good ...

Pause

The person you are speaking to understands everything ... They are reacting as you want.

Pause
Enjoy the moment.

2. Bring the class back together and ask each student to spend 10-15 minutes writing a letter to him/herself about the guided visualisation. Tell them that no one else will see the text.

3. After 15 minutes ask the students to put their letters in a large envelope and staple it shut.

Lesson 2
1. Open the envelope and give the students back their letters, allowing time for reading and then some feedback.

Note
It is well known that you can improve your performance in any sphere by re-living a time when you did something similar very well. The aim in this activity is to help bring L1 self-confidence into L2 production.

66 Writing with the Help of Music and Others

Language focus: Enriching a skeleton text

Level: Lower intermediate to advanced

Time: 50 minutes

Preparation: Bring in a CD player.

1. Say to your students:

   Sit comfortably and imagine yourself in water – in a bath or shower, a lake or the sea ... Feel the relationship between your warmth and the water temperature ... Now listen to some music and notice the pictures and feelings that come up for you.

   Play the music.

   Now write two or three sentences about the images you got, or the feeling that came over you. If you went blank, write about the blankness.
   Write your name on the paper and pass it to another student.

2. They read their neighbour's text and write one or two questions about it.

3. The papers are passed on again. Each student writes two more questions about the original text.

4. Once the papers have been passed on four times, they are returned to the original writer.

5. Each person reads the questions below their text, thinks about the answers and now writes a much fuller version of the original text, using the questions from the other students to help them to explore aspects of their experience.

6. Group students in fours to read what they have written.

Acknowledgement
We learnt this exercise from Clement Laroy, author of *Musical Openings*, Pilgrims Longman, 1993.

My Ideal Language Self

Language focus:	Writing
Level:	Intermediate to advanced
Time:	40–50 minutes
Preparation:	Make one photocopy of the worksheet for each student. Optional: bring in a CD player.

in class

1. Brainstorm all the reasons students can think of why knowing English would be useful or enjoyable for them. Be prepared to help them if they get stuck.

2. Give each student a photocopy of the following worksheet, or write it on the board and have them copy it. Let them have enough time to answer the questions thoughtfully. Help them with any language they need to express themselves.

How would knowing English better be good for me now?
How would knowing English better be good for me in the future?
How would knowing English better affect my self-confidence?
What doors would knowing English better open for me?
What tools and abilities do I have to learn more English?
What could I do to learn English better?

3. Give students a few minutes to compare their answers with someone else.

4. Ask them then to sit comfortably and close their eyes if they wish. Either play CD track no. 16 or say the following in a gentle voice, changing the script if you wish to adapt it more closely to your students' age, interests, aspirations:

Relax and observe your breathing for a few moments .... Breathe deeply and slowly ... Imagine yourself looking very far away. In the distance you see someone ... You move closer and recognise yourself a few years from now ... You are with a group of people about your age and you are speaking English to them. You are very excited about what you are saying, and everyone is listening to you with enthusiasm. Several people make comments, and you understand them perfectly, and enjoy being able to communicate with them in English about things all of you are interested in ... The group goes over to a coffee shop and you all enter and sit down. When the waiter asks in English what you want, you answer and he smiles as he writes down your order. Everyone in the group wants to know your opinion about something very important to all of you. You explain your ideas very clearly and then listen to them expressing theirs. When it is time to leave the coffee shop, you ask the waiter for your bill and you pay. Your friends want to see you again at the weekend to take a trip some place you really want to visit. As you leave, you agree on a time to meet them, and say goodbye. Now you walk towards a building where you work. In your job, you use English a lot. You enjoy what you are doing, and are very successful, and you are able to communicate well in English with people from many countries. Stay with this feeling of confidence in your abilities for a moment ... Now when you are ready, open your eyes and bring your attention back to this room, keeping with you the feeling of being able to communicate well in English.

5. To round off the activity, have each student say one word that expresses how she or he feels at the moment; start with a student you expect to express a positive feeling. Tim Murphey (1998b) explains how students are often influenced by their 'near peers', and so in any activity of this nature it is good to begin with someone who establishes a positive tone for those who follow.

6. For lower levels, to give students ideas, you could have on the board, on the OHP or computer projector a fairly complete list of adjectives expressing states such as *happy, confused, confident, pleased, capable, motivated, tired,* etc.

Variation

A further or alternative follow-up would be to discuss briefly with students the importance of setting reasonable goals. Ask them to write down one or two short-term goals regarding improving their English. They should be specific and have a deadline (e.g. to learn five new phrasal verbs a week; to speak in English outside class at least two times a week, even if only to non-native speaker friends; to watch one film or TV programme in English every weekend). Tell them that this is just for themselves, but that after three weeks you will ask them to share with their classmates if they were able to reach their goals and if they found setting the goals useful.

Note

Writing about possible selves, Dörnyei (2005) cites much research that shows that the self is dynamic – it can change. Helen Markus, professor of psychology at Stanford University, has researched with her associates the sociocultural influences on mind and self, affirming that 'imaging one's own actions through the construction of elaborated possible selves achieving the desired goal may thus directly facilitate the translation of goals into intentions and instrumental actions' (Markus and Ruvolo 1989:213). Mental images form part of the basis for our attitudes and our decision-making regarding our behaviour. So if we see the potential within ourselves, this can motivate behaviour directed towards achievement.

Three Personality Types

Language focus:	Talking about personality qualities
Level:	Intermediate to advanced
Time:	30–40 minutes
Preparation:	Make copies of the text below, one for each student. For the variation, make copies of the chart.

in class

1. Explain to the students that you are going to present three personality types to them. Their task will be to see if they know any people who correspond to the three types. Leave 1 or 2 minutes between each personality type.

2. Ask the students to sit comfortably and close their eyes if they wish. Then say:

   You are going to hear a particular type of person speaking ...
   Don't worry if you don't understand all the words ... As you listen, try to think if you know anyone like this ...

   I like to do things properly ...
   I hate making mistakes ...
   Why are some people so lazy? ...
   I live with a judge inside my head ... sometimes the judge is wise, but sometimes the judge is stern and harsh ...
   I am very, very thorough ... I work everything out carefully.
   I am a serious, no-nonsense person ...
   I always follow my conscience ... I do what I think is right ...
   My fear is the fear of being defective ... of being bad ...
   What I most want is integrity, honesty, clarity ...
   I find it hard to know when to stop correcting something I have done ...
   I pay a great price for wanting to be perfect ...
   I will now leave you some moments of silence to see ... and hear ... and feel a person you know like the person above. If you can't think of anyone you know, just try to imagine what this type of person would be like.

   Pause

   Here is a second person speaking about themselves:
   I am a thoughtful and generous person ...
   I love welcoming people and helping them ...
   It feels natural to be friendly ... I start conversations easily ...
   I get involved with others ... their dreams and hopes and needs

are more important than my own ... sometimes ...
Maybe I do more for other people than I should ...
I am both warm and supportive to people in need ...
My fear is that nobody will love me ...
I need to be needed ...
If I see a stray dog in the street, I want to bring it home ...
I am good at healing broken hearts ...
I just love being in harmony with people ...
I prefer needy people to whole people ...
I will now leave you some moments of silence to see ... hear ... and feel a person you know like the person above or one that you imagine.

Pause

Here is a third person talking about themselves:
I see myself as a highly competent person ...
It is important to me to feel successful ...
I often try to be the best at what I am doing – better than others ...
I am something of a workaholic ... I must always be doing something ...
I feel lost if I am not accomplishing things ...
When I am feeling insecure, I can be rather aloof and cool with people ...
My fear is that I am worthless and without value ...
I love to be the centre of attention and to perform ...
I sometimes want to achieve my goals the quick way ...
I often don't know what I am feeling ... my feelings seem hidden from me ...
I am effective, efficient and reliable ...
Now I will give you some moments of silence to see ... hear ... and feel a person you know like the one above or one that you imagine.

3. Bring the students back from their exploration and give out copies of the text about the three types (see next page). Have them read through the text, asking you about any words they don't understand.

4. Pair the students randomly. Ask them to decide who is A and who is B in the pair.

5. Tell them that the As have 2 minutes to tell the Bs their reactions to the activity.

6. Stop the As after 2 minutes. Now tell the Bs they have 2 minutes to give their reactions. Stop them after 2 minutes.

7. Have a general discussion about the three types:

Type 1
I like to do things properly.
I hate making mistakes.
Why are some people so lazy?
I live with a judge inside my head ... sometimes the judge is wise but sometimes the judge is stern and harsh.
I am very, very thorough. I work everything out carefully.
I am a serious, no-nonsense person.
I always follow my conscience. I do what I think is right ...
My fear is the fear of being defective ... of being bad.
What I most want is integrity, honesty, clarity.
I find it hard to know when to stop correcting something I have done.
I pay a great price for wanting to be perfect.

Type 2
I am a thoughtful and generous person.
I love welcoming people and helping them.
It feels natural to be friendly ... I start conversations easily
I get involved with others ... their dreams and hopes and needs are more important than my own sometimes.
Maybe I do more for other people than I should.
I am both warm and supportive to people in need.
My fear is that nobody will love me.
I need to be needed.
If I see a stray dog in the street, I want to bring it home.
I am good at healing broken hearts.
I just love being in harmony with people.
I prefer needy people to whole people.

Type 3
I see myself as a highly competent person.
It is important to me to feel successful.
I often try to be the best at what I am doing – better than others.
I am something of a workaholic ... I must always be doing something.
I feel lost if I am not accomplishing things.
When I am feeling insecure, I can be rather aloof and cool with people.
My fear is that I am worthless and without value.
I love to be the centre of attention and to perform.
I sometimes want to achieve my goals the quick way.
I often don't know what I am feeling ... my feelings seem hidden from me.
I am effective, efficient and reliable.

Variation
Have students work individually to decide which personality type might make each statement on the chart below. Then check their answers and discuss any points that come up. Ask them to tell their neighbour which type they feel closest to and why. Explain that these are only three of the nine types, so they may not really identify with any.

	Type 1	Type 2	Type 3
1. I am very pleased that I did that job so well.			
2. I really try to work out every little detail.			
3. Why don't you come over and tell me about your problem?			
4. I like Joan's idea, but I'm sure I can think of something better.			
5. I wonder if I made them angry with me? I hope not.			
6. Tom did terrible work on his project. He didn't make the effort.			
7. I feel bad – I don't have anything I should be doing right now.			
8. I did that because I really feel it was the correct thing to do.			
9. Let's try to find a solution that we can all be happy with.			

Answers: 1.–3; 2.–1; 3.–2; 4.–3; 5.–2; 6.–1; 7.–3; 8.–1; 9.–2

Note
This personality-type system is known as the Enneagram; you can set internet research homework for students who want to know about the other six types. The following is a useful book on the subject: *The Wisdom of the Enneagram*, by Richard Riso and Russ Hudson, Bantam Books, 1999.

69

Exploring Boredom

Language focus: From listening to writing to reading

Level: Upper intermediate to advanced

Time: 50-60 minutes

Preparation: One copy of the reading per student.

in class

1. Ask people round the room when they have been most bored in their lives.

2. Ask a student to come to the board and to act as class 'secretary'. Get the group to brainstorm words they associate with boredom … with being bored. Continue until the board is covered with words.

3. Tell the students to yawn at you and at each other … join in yourself.

4. Tell the students to sit comfortably, and to close their eyes if they want. Then say:

   I am going to ask you some questions and will pause after each one to give you time to answer it mentally:
   When was I last bored?
   What is the most boring meal I have been to?
   How long did it go on for?
   Who is the most boring person I know?
   What do they do to bore me so much?
   Who is the most boring teacher I have had?
   What did I do when I was bored in class?
   When I am bored, what happens to my inner pictures?
   When I am bored, what are my feelings?
   When I am bored, does this change the way I talk to myself?
   What is it that I do as boredom begins?
   Can being bored be a stimulus, sometimes?
   How bored am I right now?

5. Bring the students out of their thoughts, and ask them to work on their own and write a page on being bored. Give them 15 minutes for this.

6. Group them in fours to discuss their thoughts and to read their pages.

Meet the Wise Person Within You

Language focus: Asking and answering questions

Level: Lower intermediate to advanced

Time: 20–30 minutes

Preparation: Select a story about a wise person (e.g. a Sufi) or use the story here. Optional: bring in a CD player.

in class

1. Tell your students a story of a wise person, or use the story skeleton below and in your own words tell your students the story of Melric the magician.

   Once upon time – king – had magician, name Melric – Melric did all the work for king – cooked meals, repaired things etc. – Melric also did all the work for other people – one morning his magic was gone – king and people had to do their work themselves. Melric frustrated – mountains – to see his old teacher, Kra – climbed for hours – found Kra in cave – told Kra his story – Kra: You are silly – lost magic because you didn't help people – Melric: What?? I did everything for them! Kra: That's the problem. You did everything for them – now they're helpless! – Melric understood – Kra gave him magic back – Kra: You must not waste it! – Kra changed Melric into a bird – flew home to castle – saw that castle was surrounded by enemy soldiers – Melric changed them into cats – people opened castle doors – dogs chased cats away – people happy – asked Melric to do their work again – Melric: I must not waste my magic! – people started doing their work themselves – king too – And Melric? – He had to learn how to make his bed!

2. Ask your students to sit comfortably and relax. Either play CD track no. 17 or, in a calm voice, say:

   Imagine that you are standing in a wood … it's early morning on a beautiful summer's day … you can hear the birds in the trees and smell the fresh scent of the trees … the sunlight is reflected in the dewdrops on the grass …
   While you are standing there feeling the soft ground under your feet … you're becoming aware that this is a special day … and as you look up through the trees you can see a high mountain … and the blue sky above it …
   Between the trees, you see a narrow path leading up the mountain … and you're beginning to walk, now … up the mountain … at your own speed … slowly putting one foot in front of the other … while you can hear the birds … and feel the gentle wind on your skin …

You know that this mountain is just the right mountain for you ... and now you are going through the rocks ... getting higher ... and you are safe and feel fine ... you have a clear view and in the distance you can see a little cave ... as you are getting closer, you can see somebody in front of the cave. It is Kra, the wise man. Melric's teacher. He's wise, and friendly and loving. Kra has noticed you, and he's smiling at you as you're getting closer. Kra offers you a place to sit down in front of him and relax.
You know that Kra is a good listener ... and you can ask him any question that you want ... take your time to wait for the answer ... if it comes ... and go on asking questions as long as you want ...

Pause for a few minutes

It is now time to slowly say goodbye to Kra and come back to this classroom ... do this in your own time ... and take the time you need until you want to open your eyes.

3. Tell the students each to write a dialogue between themselves and Kra about any topic they like. Put the students into pairs and get them to work on the language of each other's dialogues. Each pair of students can then pass on their dialogues to another pair of students who, after 4 or 5 minutes' preparation time, are to act out one of the two dialogues of their own choice. N.B.: It is important that students really act out the dialogues, and don't just read them from the texts they've been given.

Variation
Alternatively, you could get students to write a 'silent dialogue' in pairs. Student A writes a question and passes it on to B who answers it. Then the paper is passed back to A again, who reacts to the answer in writing, etc.

Acknowledgements
The activity is based on Piero Ferrucci's 'Inner dialogue' activity. *What we may be: The visions and techniques of Psychosynthesis.* Turnstone Press Ltd., 1982 p. 144.
The story of Melric is based on a beautiful children's book by David McKee, *The Magician who Lost his Magic*, Abelard-Schuman, London, 1970.

71 The Magic Ring

Language focus:	The conditional; writing
Level:	Intermediate to advanced
Time:	30–40 minutes
Preparation:	None.

in class

1. Tell your students to sit comfortably and try to see in their minds a story in which they are the main character:

   You are strolling down a street in an old part of a very old city ... It is a foggy winter night and you are all alone. You are enjoying this walk a lot, the interesting and somewhat mysterious old buildings, the smell of smoke from the fires burning in fireplaces, the cold air, the silence of the night ... Suddenly you see something shining on the ground ... You bend down and pick it up ... it is a golden ring. You take it and rub it against your sleeve. Even at night it shines very brightly. You try it on ... it fits you perfectly and a strange sensation spreads throughout your body. It is wonderful, and you feel like the most powerful person in the world. You remember you haven't had dinner and you are very hungry ... you feel you would like a piece of chocolate cake and suddenly there it is ... in your hand. At that moment, you realise that all your dreams can come true.

   What would you do with this magnificent power?

   Think carefully about it, consider the world situation, your own life, and the lives of others you know, and remember that you can do everything – whatever you want. Decide on what you would like to do with this power, picture it in your mind.

2. After 2–3 minutes, quietly invite students to write down how they would answer the question about what they would do if they had this power. Give them 15 minutes to write.

3. In pairs they tell their partner what they would do. Then between them they negotiate three things they would both want to do.

4. Have each pair share their three things with the rest of the class.

Acknowledgement
This activity is adapted from Javier Ávila (2002).

72 Positive Qualities

Language focus: Lexical set of positive qualities; introducing oneself

Level: Elementary to advanced

Time: 20 minutes

Preparation: Bring in a CD player.
Computer projector presentation, or photocopies of chart.

in class 1. Revise ways to introduce oneself in English.

2. Pre-teach some of the words dealing with positive qualities that your students might not know.

POSITIVE QUALITIES

love

harmony   beauty

goodness

compassion   understanding

confidence   courage

cooperation   friendship

determination   order   discipline

stability   serenity

happiness   joy

gratitude   appreciation

generosity   light

energy   enthusiasm   vitality

humility   patience

loyalty   freedom

optimism   peace

wisdom

3. Project the Positive Qualities slide or use photocopies of the chart. If you use a computer projector you can bring the lines up one at a time, pausing slightly between each line. Ask your students if there are any qualities that are important for them that they would like to add to the list, and write these on the board. Have them each write down five that they feel are very important for them, and share these with a partner.

4. Playing the music, invite students to sit comfortably and relax. Then say in a quiet voice:

   Decide on one of the qualities that you would really like to have or to have more of. Maybe patience, maybe friendliness, maybe courage ... You decide ...

   See yourself as having this quality in your life ... How would you feel? ... What would you do that would be different from now? ... How would you relate to other people? .... How might your life change? ... See your face, your body, the way you move ... See an image of yourself having this quality fully developed in you ... Enjoy this image for a minute ....

5. Then tell them that they going to get up and move around and introduce themselves to several of their classmates, shaking their hand and saying their name and adding their quality as their surname: 'Hello, I'm Ana Cooperation,' or, 'Hi, I'm Pierre Enthusiasm,' or, 'My name is Maria Freedom,' They can create little dialogues like the following:
   María: Hello, I'm María Freedom.
   Pierre: Nice to meet you María; I'm Pierre Enthusiasm.
   María: I'm pleased to meet you.

Note
This works best with a warmed-up group. There is a nice contrast between the serious inwardness of the first part and the movement and laughter in the final part.

Acknowledgement
This activity is adapted from Whitmore (1986).

Drawing an Image of You

Language focus:	Speaking
Level:	Lower intermediate to advanced
Time:	30 minutes
Preparation:	Optional: the painting for the computer projector, or printed for students to see.

1. Brainstorm words related to painting. Be sure the students know *drawings, canvas, brushes.*

2. Ask the students to take out a piece of paper and a pen or pencil. Show them the painting of an artist's studio if you wish, and then tell them the following:

   Sit comfortably and relax, close your eyes if you wish ... Imagine you are an artist and you have a room in your home where you paint. Sometimes you paint very complex works, and other times you make funny little drawings. But you know that no matter how you decide to paint, you can express what you want to say in your paintings ... You are going to begin a new painting, and in it you want to express the most important things about yourself ... Imagine now what you will put in your painting ... What places will you include? ... What people? ... What things? ... What symbols can you use to express your most important values? ... Think about all these aspects to include in your painting for a moment ...

   Now come back ... but not to this room. Come back in your imagination to the place where you paint. You have your pencils to draw with, your paints, your brushes .... There is a fresh canvas waiting for you .... But first on a piece of paper you want to draw what you plan to paint on the canvas later. This is not about perfect drawing; it is about expressing something about you.

3. Get the students to do their drawings, and then work in pairs and show the drawings to their partner. They can ask each other questions about what they have included, what the drawings represent, why they are important for them. You can go around the room looking at their drawings too, asking questions and making some positive comments.

Drawing an Image of You

Variations

1. You may want to collect the drawings and stick them up on the walls, and have students walk around, trying to guess who made the drawings.

2. Another option is to give each student someone else's drawings and have them create a description of the person from the drawings.

74 A New You

Language focus: Language of description

Level: Elementary to advanced

Time: 30–40 minutes

Preparation: One photocopy of the worksheet for each student.

in class

1. Write the following questions on the board:
   Who are you?
   Where do you live?
   What do you want to do in life?

2. In pairs, preferably mixing up students so they don't work with someone they know well, student A asks B each question, but after B answers, A repeats the same question four more times, so B answers each question a total of five times. You can demonstrate this, so they can see how each time you have to think a little more to find an answer. A asks the second question and the third, getting five answers for each. Then B asks A the three questions in the same way.

3. Say to students:
   Try to remember when you were a child and were playing, who did you sometimes pretend you were ... a cowboy ... a princess ... a doctor ... a singer? ... Try to see yourself as a child pretending to be someone else.
   Pretend now that you could be anything you would like to be, have any situation and any qualities you want, a new identity ... Take a moment to imagine a new you. Where would you live? ... what kind of work would you have? what things would you do in your free time? ... what special qualities would you have? ...

4. Give out the worksheet and have students complete it on their own, inventing a new identity, even their name and age. When they have finished filling it in, get everyone to stand up and go around the room meeting other students, asking and answering questions about themselves in their new identity.

Variation
In pairs after reading each other's worksheet, they prepare a role-play of this situation: You are seated by a person you don't know on an airplane and you want to get to know them, to have someone to talk to during the flight. They prepare a short conversation in their new roles to perform for the rest of the class.

Note
An important part of Lozanov's Suggestopedic language–teaching method is taking on an attractive new identity. It has been said this can encourage learners to take more risks in speaking because they are acting the role of 'John, the famous journalist' or 'Felicia the film star' and so they can leave their own inhibitions behind.

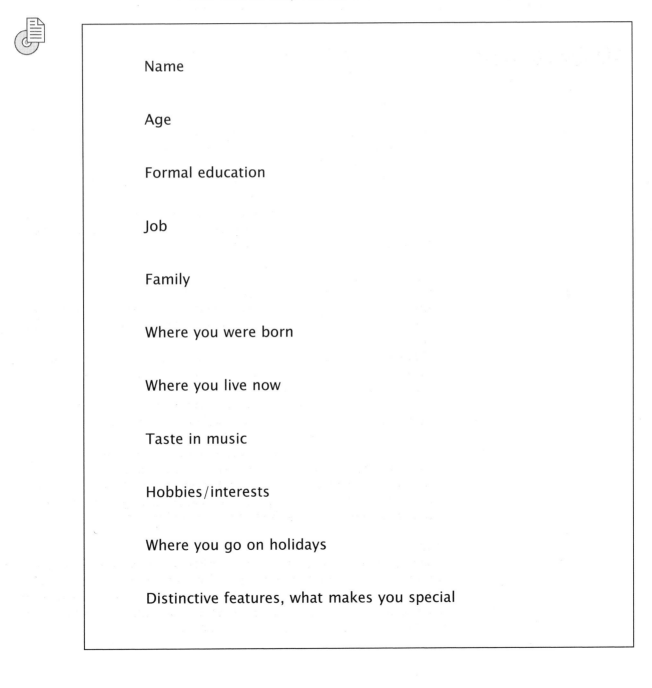

Name

Age

Formal education

Job

Family

Where you were born

Where you live now

Taste in music

Hobbies/interests

Where you go on holidays

Distinctive features, what makes you special

75 Our Group

Language focus:	Speaking
Level:	Intermediate to advanced
Time:	40–50 minutes
Preparation:	Make cards with sayings (see end of activity), one for every two students. If you have a larger class, you can find more sayings or repeat some. Cut the sayings cards in half. One photocopy of the interview scheme (overleaf) for each student.

in class

1. Have students brainstorm some values – suggest a few (*honesty, tolerance* ...) to help them think, and also write these on the board. (If you have recently done Activity 72, Positive Qualities, you can leave out this step.)

2. Then have them brainstorm types of groups they have been in or know of – a class, club, family etc. Write these on the board. Have them bring to mind a group that has been really good for them.

3. To get students in random pairs, give each of them half of a sayings card. Students walk around trying to find someone with the other half of their saying; when they do, they sit down together.

4. Tell them that in a minute they are going to interview each other about a good group they have been in. They will try to get a clear image of the group in their mind. Have them decide who is A and who is B in each pair. As will interview Bs first. Tell them there are two parts to the interview: first they will discuss something positive about themselves, and then they will explore the good group they know. The interviewers should encourage the person who is speaking, but not interrupt them. They should ask their questions slowly, and give their partner time to think and to answer thoughtfully.

Our Group

Interview scheme

Part I
Ask your partner the following questions. Give them enough time to answer the first one before you go on to the next.

· *If I asked some people who know you well what some of the good things about you are, what would they say?*

· *What values are important for you?*

Part II
Think of a time when you were in a really good group. See this group in your mind. Think about what it was like to be in the group. Tell me about this. Pause for your partner to begin. If they need help ask more questions such as the following. *Tell me more. How did you feel in the group? What made you feel that way? What made the group work so well?*

---

5. When they have finished, change roles and Bs interview As. When they have had time to complete the second interview, bring the class together and brainstorm what they find are some of the things that characterise a good group. Write them on the board, and discuss them. Get the students to make suggestions for making their class a good group.

Note
It is useful to do the activity towards the beginning of the term to start with a productive group atmosphere. Hadfield (1992) and Dörnyei and Murphey (2003), among others, have pointed out the importance of developing a good group climate for better classroom language learning.

The format of the activity is adapted from the Appreciative Inquiry dialogue (see Cooperrider 2001). We have used it with classes that need to work together on group projects in order to establish an awareness of the importance of group coherence and of what makes a group work well. Students often complain that when working in groups some people do all the work while others go for a free ride. Group consciousness–raising can help avoid that situation and develop a commitment from all members.

75 Our Group

Sayings cards

If you think you can	or think you can't … you are right.
In all things we only learn	from those we love.
The first step to wisdom is silence	the second is listening.
Problems are what you see	when you take your eyes off your goal.
They may forget what you said but they	will never forget how you made them feel.
A good beginning makes	a good end.
Everything you can imagine	is real.
If you are not happy	here and now, you will never be happy.
Only in the darkness	can you see the stars.
You should be the change you	want to see in the world.
Try first to understand, then	to be understood.
The mind is like a parachute; it	only works when it is open.
If you can't be a poet,	be a poem.
You don't become what you think,	you become what you believe.

76 Get Away

Language focus: Writing, listening and speaking

Level: Lower intermediate to advanced

Time: 20–30 minutes

Preparation: None.

in class

1. Explain to students the importance of knowing how to avoid stress – for learning in general, for exam situations in particular, for good health and many other reasons. Tell them you are going to give them a tool to use whenever they want. Have them sit comfortably and in a quiet voice say:

   Observe your breathing for a moment, notice how when you breathe in deeply you bring a feeling of calm, and when you breathe out, your worries and problems become smaller and even disappear ... Now, to help you relax more, think of a place that for you is very peaceful. It may be a real place that you know or it may be a wonderful place you imagine ... I'm going to give you a few moments to be in this place, to observe everything that is there, to experience completely what you see, what you hear, what you smell, what you feel there. Enjoy being in this place.

   Pause for 3 to 4 minutes.

   Now you are going to come back to the classroom, but remember you can return to this place in your mind whenever you want to relax and feel better.

2. Now ask your students to remember their chosen place and to write a description of it in the form of a guided visit to the place. Give them a basic scheme such as the following, to use some or all of:

   *I want you to imagine you are walking in/at/through/up (place)...
   It is a (......) day in (season)... It is (time of day)...
   You can see ... There are ... You can also see ... Now you come to ...
   As you walk, you can hear ...*

3. Encourage them to use all their senses and to bring in as many details as they can. Have them suggest things that a visitor there might want to do. As they write, you can walk around the room helping with any language doubts, but stress that the writing should be clear and quite simple.

4. When they finish, have them work in pairs and, speaking slowly and quietly, guide each other through their special place. When As finish, Bs should thank them for the visit, and then Bs guide the As through their place. When both have done the exercise, have them talk about how it went for them

Note

After the activity, you might remind your students of the importance of being more relaxed, and invite them to breathe deeply and return to their special place just for a minute two or three times a day. Marc Helgesen (personal communication) comments that in his university department in Japan they teach students this type of skill, and encourage them to make use of it in exams, job interviews and so forth.

Imagine ... an Ideal World

Imagine all those people ... living life in peace. John Lennon

Language focus: Speaking and writing

Level: Lower intermediate to advanced

Time: 15 minutes, then two periods of 40–50 minutes

Preparation: Photocopies of the worksheet.
Optional: if you have a recording of John Lennon's *Imagine*, bring it in, with a CD player, to play while students are working individually in Lesson 1.

This activity is designed to be done as project work

Lesson 1
1. Using the cooperative learning structure Think-Pair-Share (Kagan: 1994), ask your students first to write down individually all the good things about the world they can think of. Then they compare lists with a partner. Only after they have had a chance to think on their own and to speak with just one person do you ask them to 'go public' and share ideas with the whole class. You can write their suggestions on the board, either as they come or grouping them into categories.

2. For the next class ask students to think about what would be their ideal world. Have them imagine in detail what this world would be like. To guide them, give each one a copy of the worksheet 'My Ideal World' to fill in.

Lesson 2
1. In self-chosen or teacher-assigned groups of three or four, students compare their ideal worlds and negotiate a single version which combines things from all of them. They then decide how to present their ideal world to the rest of the class. Some suggestions you give them might include: a song, a poem, a story, a role-play, a computer projector presentation, a poster with drawings or photos and text, an essay, a letter from someone living in the ideal world ... They will have several days to work on this outside class, and time to ask for your corrections and help before they present their project.

Lesson 3
1. The groups present their projects to the rest of the class.

Variation
Instead of working on this topic as a project, after Lesson 1 each student hands in a composition based on the notes taken on the worksheet.

Imagine ... an Ideal World

Imagine all those people ... living life in peace. John Lennon

Note
With Appreciative Inquiry (Cooperrider 2001), it is stressed that the best way to begin to deal with any situation is to start with the positive. This involves a shift in emphasis from looking first at problems to looking at achievements, thinking about what is working instead of what isn't. It uses the energy for change from past successes to promote future developments. There is a powerful generative force in the images of excellence we hold. In this activity we start with the positive that students know of the world.

> MY IDEAL WORLD
> Make some notes of your ideas
>
> If I imagine my ideal world, some of the things I would like to see or see more of are:
>
> Some things I would like to eliminate are:
>
> As I imagine my ideal world, I see these differences in people's lives:
>
> I see cities like this:
>
> I see the country, sea, mountains, forests, etc. like this:
>
> In my ideal world I see myself as:

References

Alesandrini, K. L. 1985. Imagery research with adults: Implications for education. In Sheikh A. and Sheikh K. (eds.) *Imagery in Education.* Farmingdale, NY: Baywood.

Arnold, J. 1999. Visualization: language learning with the mind's eye. In Arnold J. (ed.), *Affect in Language Learning.* Cambridge: Cambridge University Press.

Arnold, J. 2000. Seeing through listening comprehension exam anxiety, *TESOL Quarterly,* 34/4, 777–786.

Avila, J. 2002. La activación de la inteligencia espacial: las imágenes mentales en el aula de inglés. In Fonseca, C. *Inteligencias múltiples: Múltiples formas de enseñar inglés.* Seville: Mergablum.

Brown, H. D. 1991. *Breaking the Language Barrier.* Yarmouth, ME: Intercultural Press.

Cooperrider, D. 2001. Positive image, positive action: The affirmative basis of organizing. In Cooperrider, D., Sorensen, P., Yaeger, T., and Whitney, D. (eds.) *Appreciative Inquiry: An Emerging Direction for Organization Development.* Champaign IL: Stipes Publishing. Or http://www.stipes.com/aichap2.htm

Damasio, A. 1994. *Descartes' Error: Emotion, Reason and the Human Brain.* New York: Avon.

Damasio, A. 2000. *The Feeling of What Happens: Body, Emotion and the Making of Consciousness.* London: Vintage.

Dewey, J. My Pedagogic Creed. http://www.infed.org/archives/e-texts/e-dew-pc.htm. First published in 1897, *The School Journal,* LIV/3, 77–80.

Dörnyei, Z. 2001. *Motivational Strategies in the Language Classroom.* Cambridge: Cambridge University Press.

Dörnyei, Z. 2005. *The Psychology of the Language Learner.* Mahwah, N: Lawrence Erlbaum Associates.

Dörnyei, Z. and Murphey, T. 2003. *Group Dynamics in the Language Classroom.* Cambridge: Cambridge University Press.

Eisner, E 1992. The misunderstood role of the arts in human development. *Phi Delta Kappan,* 591–595.

Gallwey, T. 1972. *The Inner Game of Tennis.* Bantam Books. Reissue edition (1984).

Gardner, H. 1993. *Frames of Mind: The Theory of Multiple Intelligences.* Second edition. London: Fontana Press.

Grinder, M. 1991. *Righting the Educational Conveyor Belt.* Portland, Oregon: Metamorphous Press.

Hadfield, C. and J. 1998. Working with (un)limited resources. *English Teaching Professional*, 7, 11.

Hadfield, J. 1992. *Classroom Dynamics.* Oxford: Oxford University Press.

Houston, J. 1982. *The Possible Human. A Course in Enhancing your Physical, Mental and Creative Abilities.* Los Angeles: J. P. Tarcher.

Kagan, S. 1994. *Cooperative Learning.* San Juan Capistrano, CA: Kagan Cooperative Learning.

Kosslyn, C. 1980. *Image and Mind.* Cambridge, Mass: Harvard University Press.

Kosslyn, C., Behrmann, M., & Jeannerod, M. 1995. The cognitive neuroscience of mental imagery. *Neuropsychologia*, 33, 11, 1335–1344.

Majoy, P. 1993. *Doorways to Learning: A Model for Developing the Brain's Full Potential.* Tucson, AR; Zephyr Press.

Markus, H., and Ruvolo, A. 1989. Possible selves: Personalized representations of goals. In L.A. Pervin (ed.) *Goal Concepts in Personality and Social Psychology* (pp. 211–241). Hillsdale, NJ; Lawrence Erlbaum Associates.

McLeod, S. 1997. *Notes on the Heart: Affective Issues in the Writing Classroom.* Carbondale: Southern Illinois University Press.

Mind Gym. 2005. *The Mind Gym: Wake your Mind Up.* London: Time Warner.

Murdock, M. 1987. *Spinning Inward: Using Guided Imagery with Children for Learning, Creativity and Relaxation.* Boston: Shambala.

Murphey, T. 1998a. Image streaming. *English Teaching Professional,* October, 9–10.

Murphey, T. 1998 b. Motivating with Near Peer Role Models. *On JALT '97: Trends & Transitions.* http://www2.dokkyo.ac.jp/~esemi029/articles/nprm.html.

Paivio, A. 1986. *Mental Representations: A Dual Coding Approach.* New York: Oxford University Press.

Puchta, H., and Rinvolucri, M. 2005. *Multiple Intelligences in EFL.* Innsbruck: Helbling Languages.

Revell, J., and Norman, S. 1997. *In Your Hands: NLP in ELT.* London: Saffire Press.

Sadoski, M., and Paivio, A. 2000. *Imagery and Text: A Dual-Coding Theory of Reading and Writing.* Mahwah, NJ: Lawrence Erlbaum Associates.

Stevick, E. 1986. *Images and Options in the Language*

Classroom. Cambridge: Cambridge University Press.

Stevick, E. 1996. *Memory, Meaning and Method.* Second edition. Boston: Heinle & Heinle.

Thornbury, S. 1999. Lesson art and design. *ELT Journal,* 53, 1, 4–11.

Tomlinson, B. 1994. Materials for TPR. Folio 1/2, 8–10.

Tomlinson B. and Avila, J. 2007a. Seeing and saying for yourself: The roles of audio–visual mental aids in language learning and use. In Tomlinson, B. (ed.) *Language Acquisition and Development: Studies of First and Other Language Learners.* London: Continuum.

Tomlinson, B. and Avila, J. 2007b. Applications of the research into the roles of audio–visual mental aids for language teaching pedagogy. In Tomlinson, B. (ed.) *Language Acquisition and Development: Studies of First and Other Language Learners.* London: Continuum.

Underhill, A. 1994. *Sound Foundations.* Oxford: Heinemann.

Wallis, C. 2006. The multitasking generation. *Time,* March 27, 48–55.

Whitmore, D. 1986. *Pyschosynthesis in Education: a Guide to the Joy of Learning.* Wellingborough: Turnstone Press Limited.

Williams, M. and Burden, R. 1997. *Psychology for Language Teachers.* Cambridge: Cambridge University Press.

Yashima, T., Zenuk-Nishide, L., and Shimizu, K. 2004. The influence of attitudes and affect on willingness to communicate and second language communication. *Language Learning,* 54(1), 119–152.

Zimmerman, S. and Keene, E.O. 1997. *Mosaic of Thought: Teaching Comprehension in a Reader's Workshop.* Portsmouth, NH: Heinemann.

Teacher's quick-reference guide

To use this chart, decide on the lesson-time available to you, and find it in the left-hand column. Then look across the grid till you reach the column showing the standard of your students. (Or start with your students and work down to the time.)

Any filled cell you reach gives you a suitable activity. And in that same row, the cell in the right-hand column indicates where you'll find it.

NB The first time you run each of these activities it may take a little longer than shown, especially when you and your students are becoming used to a new way of working.

LESSON TIME (IN MINS)	Activity	Levels	SECTION	ACTIVITY
2/any time	Visual error correction	Elementary–Advanced	2	26
3-5	From touch to inner picture	Elementary–Advanced	1	5
5	The irregular-verbs gym	Elementary–Advanced	2	28
5-10	The kitten on your lap	Elementary–Advanced	1	2
5-10	From movement to inner picture	Elementary–Advanced	1	6
5-10	Seeing colours and numbers	Elementary–Advanced	1	8
5-10	Flipping a picture over	Elementary–Advanced	2	22
5-10	What have I learnt today?	Elementary–Advanced	2	27
5-15	Point to where the window is	Elementary–Lower Int.	1	1
10-15	Shapes in spaces	Elementary–Intermediate	4	55
15	Letting the images flow	Lower Int.–Advanced	4	50
15-20	Your own name	Elementary–Advanced	1	10
15-20	Revising vocabulary using images	Elementary–Advanced	2	21
15-20	Going up in a balloon	Lower Int.–Intermediate	4	53
20	Come to your senses	Elementary–Advanced	1	4
20	The dreamer within me	Intermediate–Advanced	1	13
20	Speak, listen and draw	Lower Int.–Advanced	2	31
20	Always someone to talk to	Elementary–Advanced	2	33
20	The time machine	Intermediate–Advanced	4	60
20	Positive qualities	Elementary–Advanced	5	72
20-30	Getting a picture in mind	Elementary–Advanced	1	9
20-30	Washing your hands	Upper Int.–Advanced	1	11
20-30	Rotating sentences in your mind	Elementary–Advanced	2	23
20-30	Expanding a story	Intermediate–Advanced	3	36
20-30	Dreaming your way into a story's vocabulary	Elementary–Lower Int.	3	39
20-30	My favourite places	Elementary–Advanced	4	49
20-30	From sound to picture: a building site	Intermediate–Advanced	4	61
20-30	Meet the wise person within you	Lower Int.–Advanced	5	70
20-30	Get Away	Lower Int.–Advanced	5	76
25-35	Elesnakes and zebradiles	Lower Int.–Advanced	2	17
30	Cooperative descriptions	Elementary–Advanced	2	32
30	The story of a mouse	Lower Int.–Advanced	3	40
30	A day in the life of ...	Lower Int.–Advanced	3	42
30	The end of the story	Elementary–Advanced	3	45
30	Night-time experiences	Lower Int.–Advanced	4	57

LESSON TIME (IN MINS)	ELEMENTARY	LOWER INT.	INTERMEDIATE	UPPER INT.	ADVANCED	SECTION	ACTIVITY
30		Drawing an image of you →					5	73
30-40	Internalising a poem in three ways (all levels)					1	7
30-40			Your very own inner film centre			1	12
30-40	Doubling a picture (all levels)					2	15
30-40	Pronouns and the reality they refer to (all levels)					2	18
30-40	The present perfect in images (all levels)					2	20
30-40			A recipe			2	24
30-40		Remember then				4	51
30-40	There was a bright, bright universe (all levels)					4	59
30-40			Me in the future			5	63
30-40			Three personality types			5	68
30-40			The magic ring			5	71
30-40	A new you (all levels)					5	74
30-50		Best friends				5	62
30-60	What kind of parent? (all levels)					3	44
35-40	Living the seasons (all levels)					4	58
40	Images to poem					2	30
40			From listening to reading to writing			3	35
40	Starting from spaces					4	52
40-50			Look inside			1	14
40-50			Learning a word with its family and friends			2	16
40-50			Getting ready for reading			2	29
40-50	From sounds to mumblings to stories (all levels)					3	37
40-50			Creating a story			3	38
40-50	A nose for bread (all levels)					3	41
40-50		Writing from the sound of music				3	46
40-50		Guided writing				3	47
40-50		The lake in the wood				4	54
45-50			What's happiness?			5	64
40-50			My ideal language self			5	67
40-50			Our group			5	75
50		Writing with the help of music and others				5	66
50-60			Floating translation			2	19
50-60			Dreamy listening			2	25

LESSON TME (IN MINS)	ELEMENTARY	LOWER INT.	INTERMEDIATE	UPPER INT.	ADVANCED	SECTION / ACTIVITY	
50-60				Exploring boredom		5	69
5 + 20-30		Where animals live				4	56
15 + 15	Questions about a picture					1	3
15-20 + 5-10		Automatic writing				2	34
25-35 + 5-10		Mother tongue as a resource state				5	65
40-50 + 10			Living my day again			3	43
40-50 + 15-30		Writing from illustrations				3	48
15 + 40-50 + 40-50		Imagine ... an ideal world				5	77

The CD / CD-ROM

The CD accompanying this book has two parts:
1. CD-ROM with
    - Text files containing worksheets and texts for use in class.
    - Files containing all the artwork from the activities in the book.
In both cases you can print the material out, transfer in onto OHTs
or convert it into PowerPoint files.

2. Audio files with
    1 a selection of taped imagery-scripts from the activities.
    2 music tracks to be used as part of some activities or to
       accompany your own reading of imagery-scripts from the book.
All the audio files can be played directly from your computer or from
a CD player.
The following icons in the book will help you with selecting files:

Further recordings of scripts and music for activities 12, 13, 17, 40,
49, 50, 63, 68 and 76 can be downloaded from the Helbling
Languages website:
www.helblinglanguages.com/imaginethat